Color My Wings ~ Coloring Book

By Cathy Allsiets

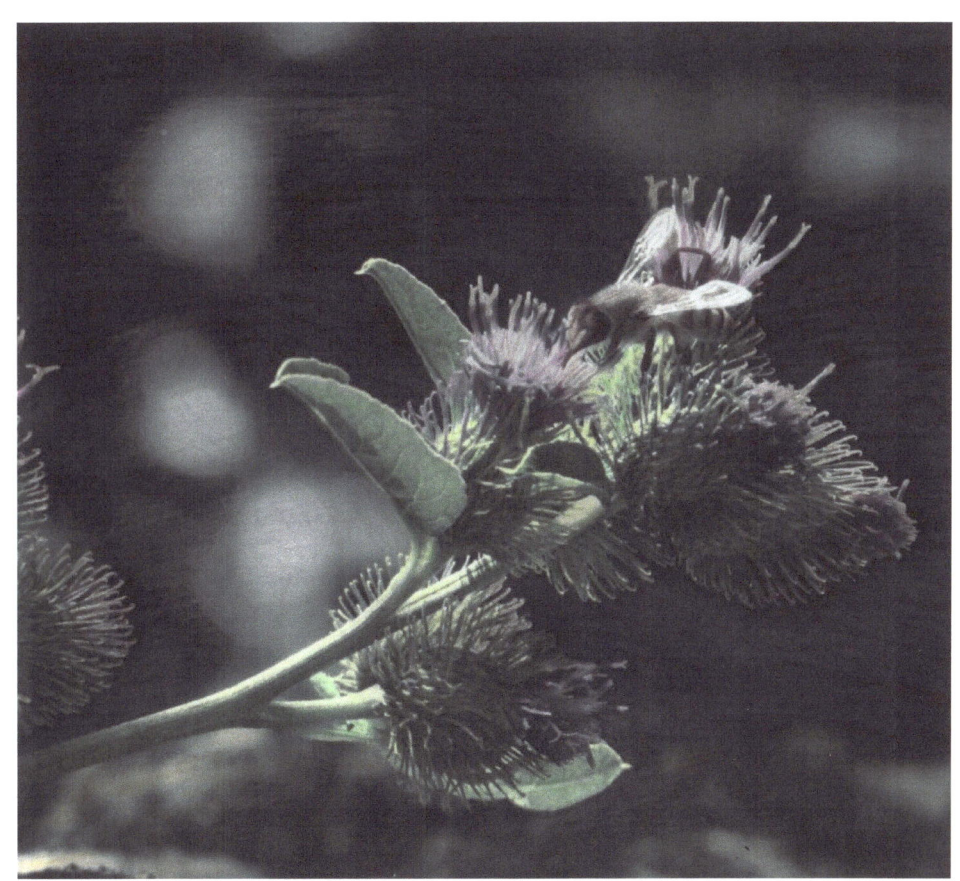

All Rights Reserved

Copyright 2017 by Cathy Allseits

No part of this book may be reproduced or transmitted, downloaded, distributed, reverse engineered, or stored in or introduced into any information storage and retrieval system, in any form or by any means, Including photocopying and recording, whether electronic or mechanical now known or hereinafter invested without permission in writing from the author.

Cathy Allseits

Via Adua, 4/A

Bra (CN) 12042

Italy

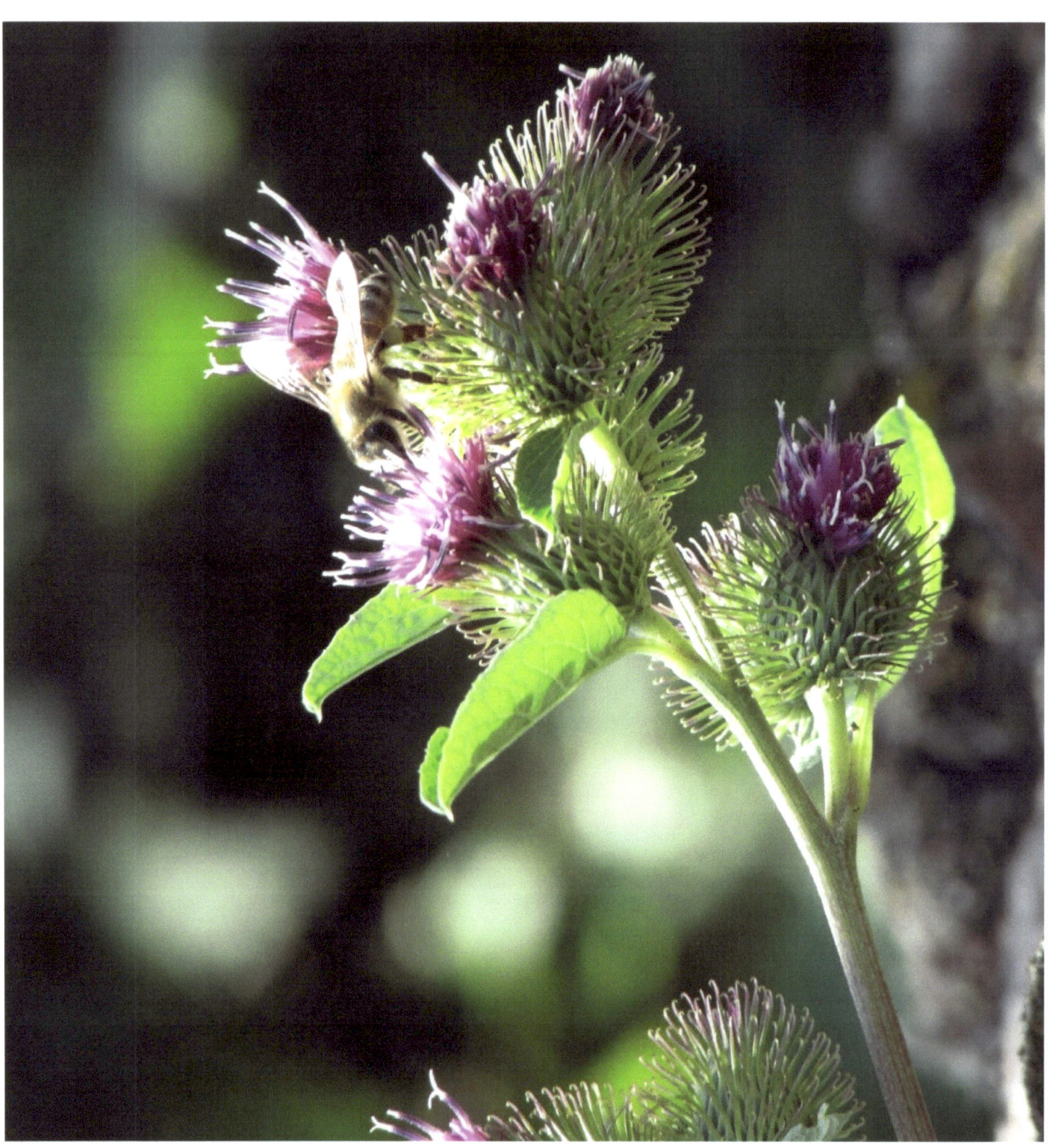

P1

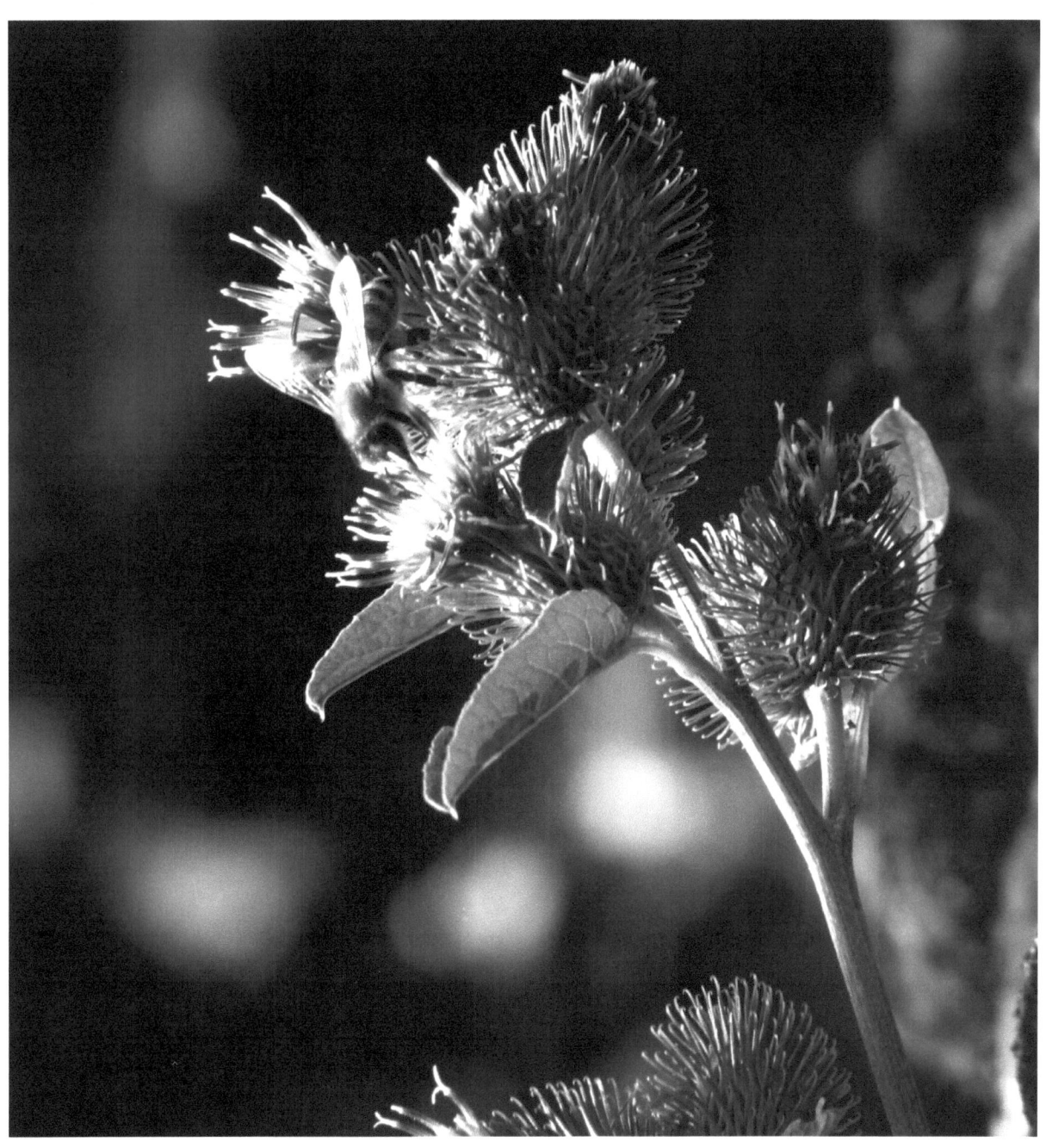

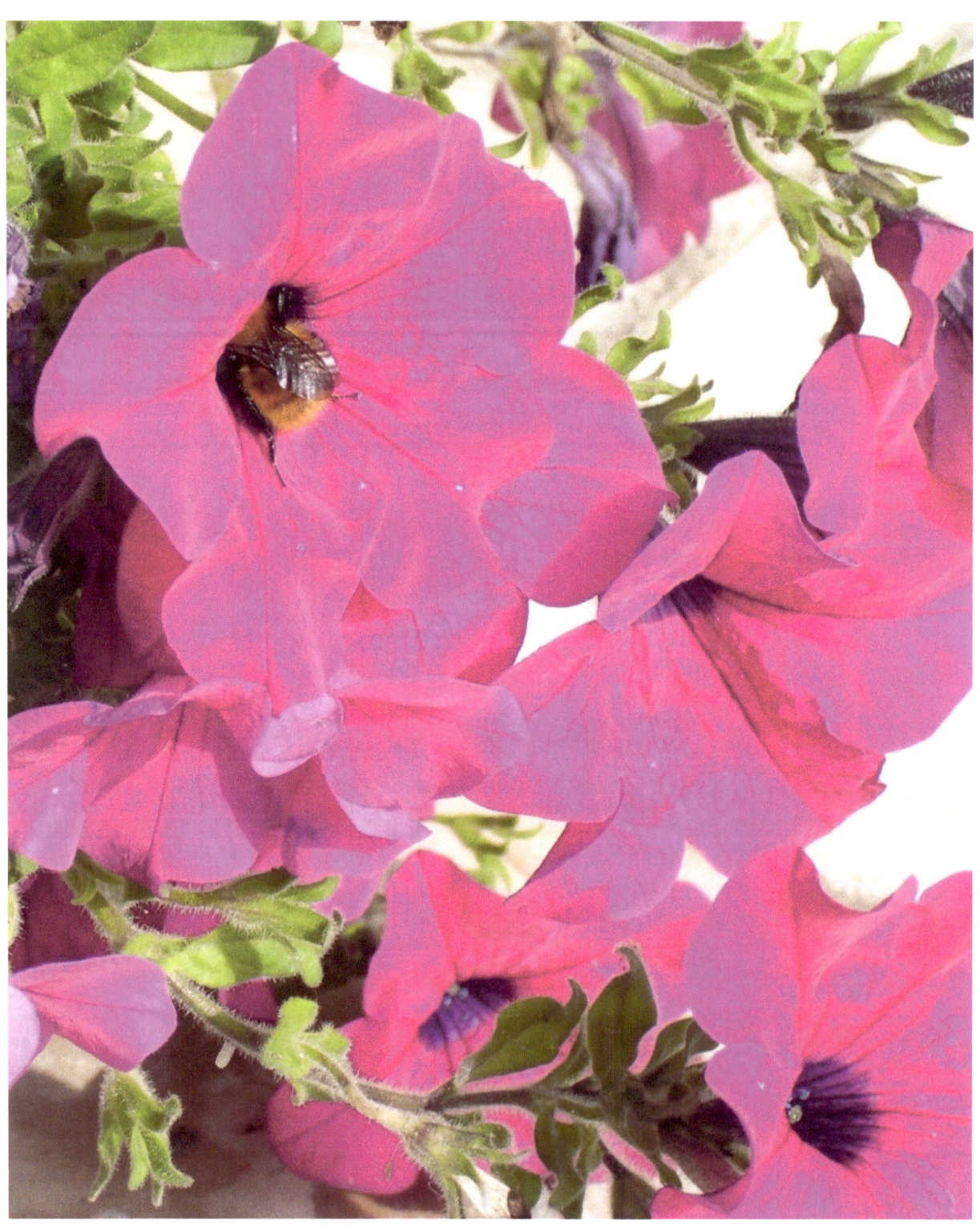

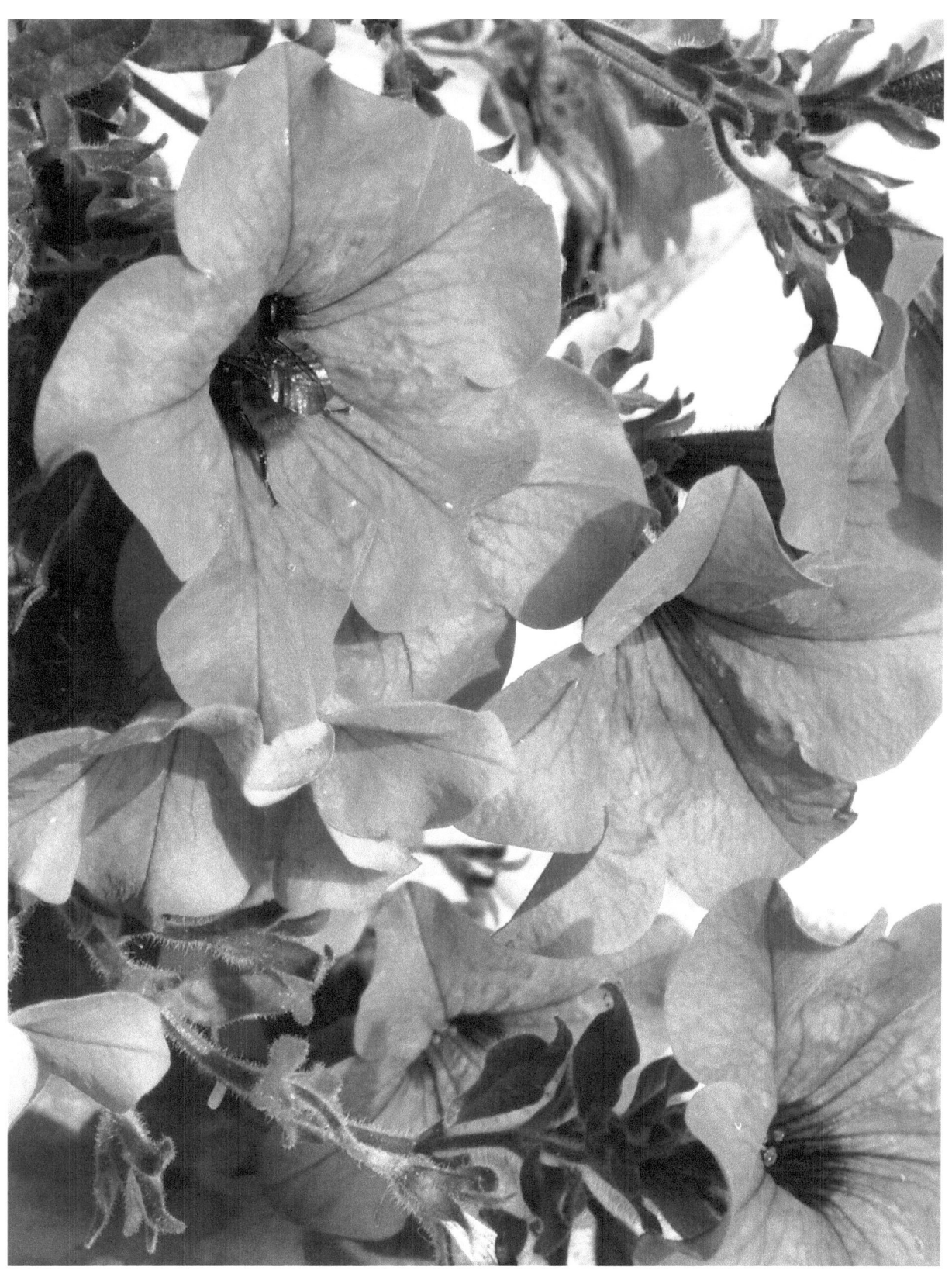

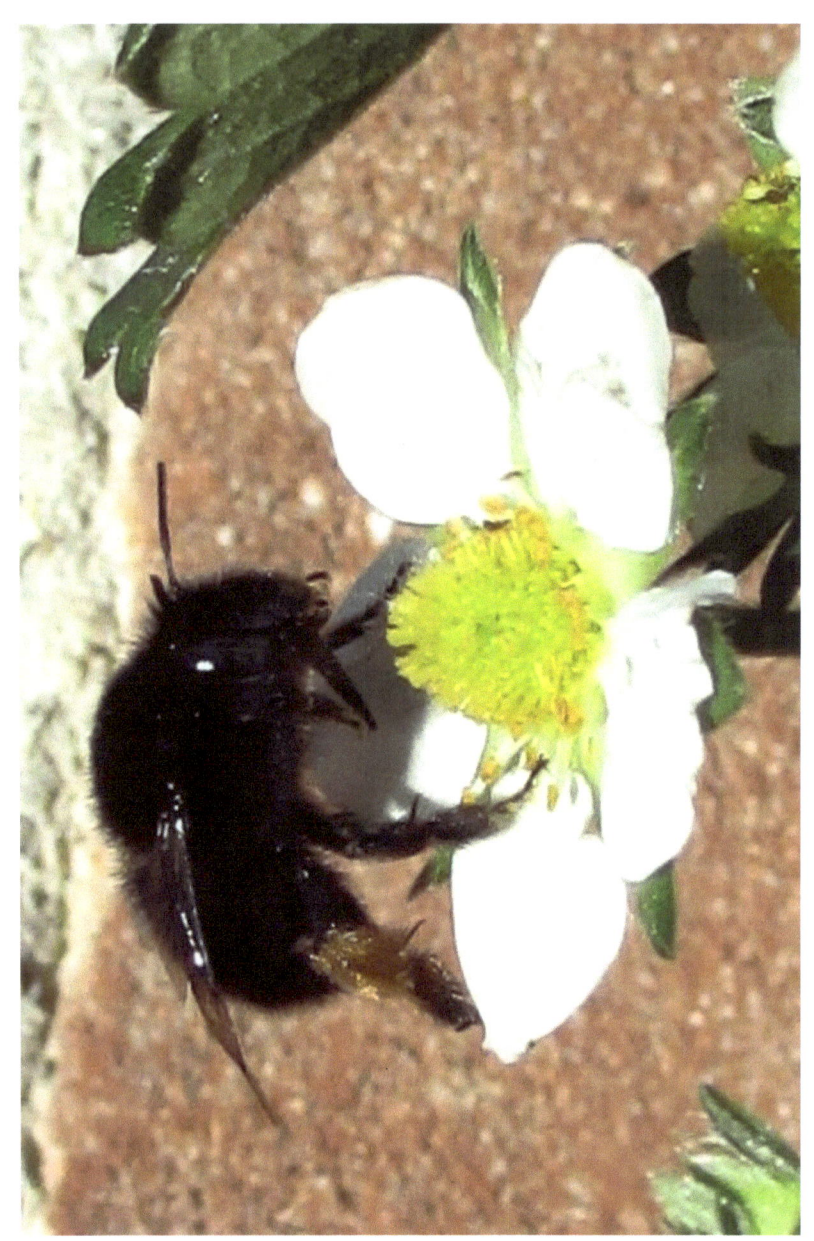

P 5

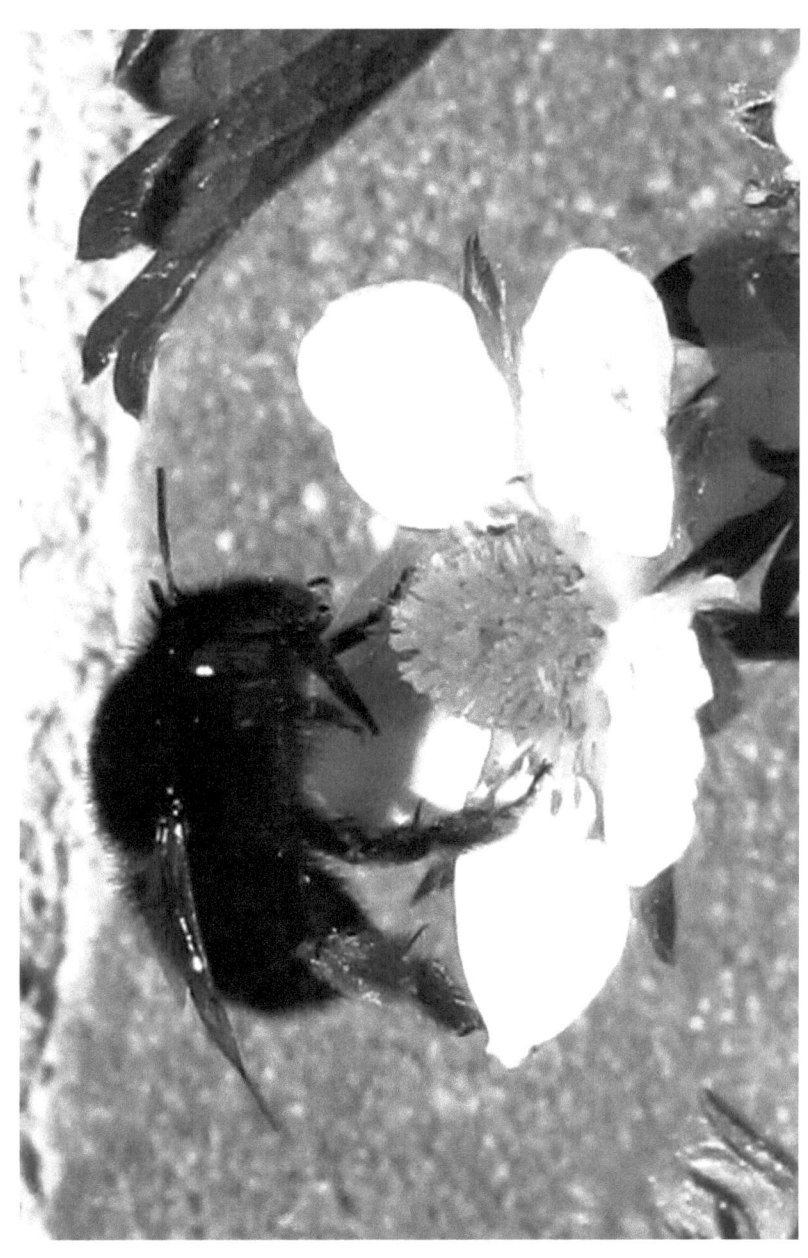

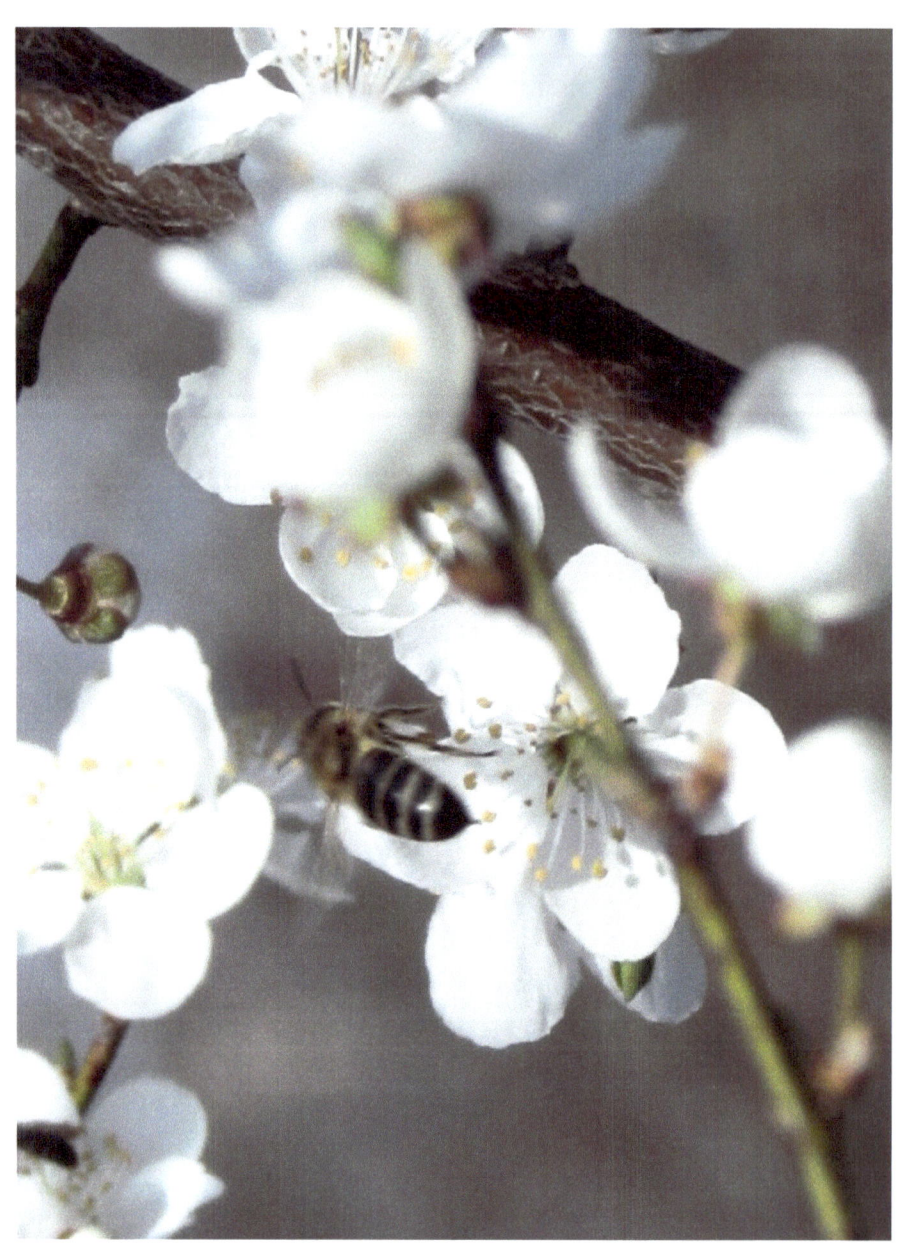

P 7

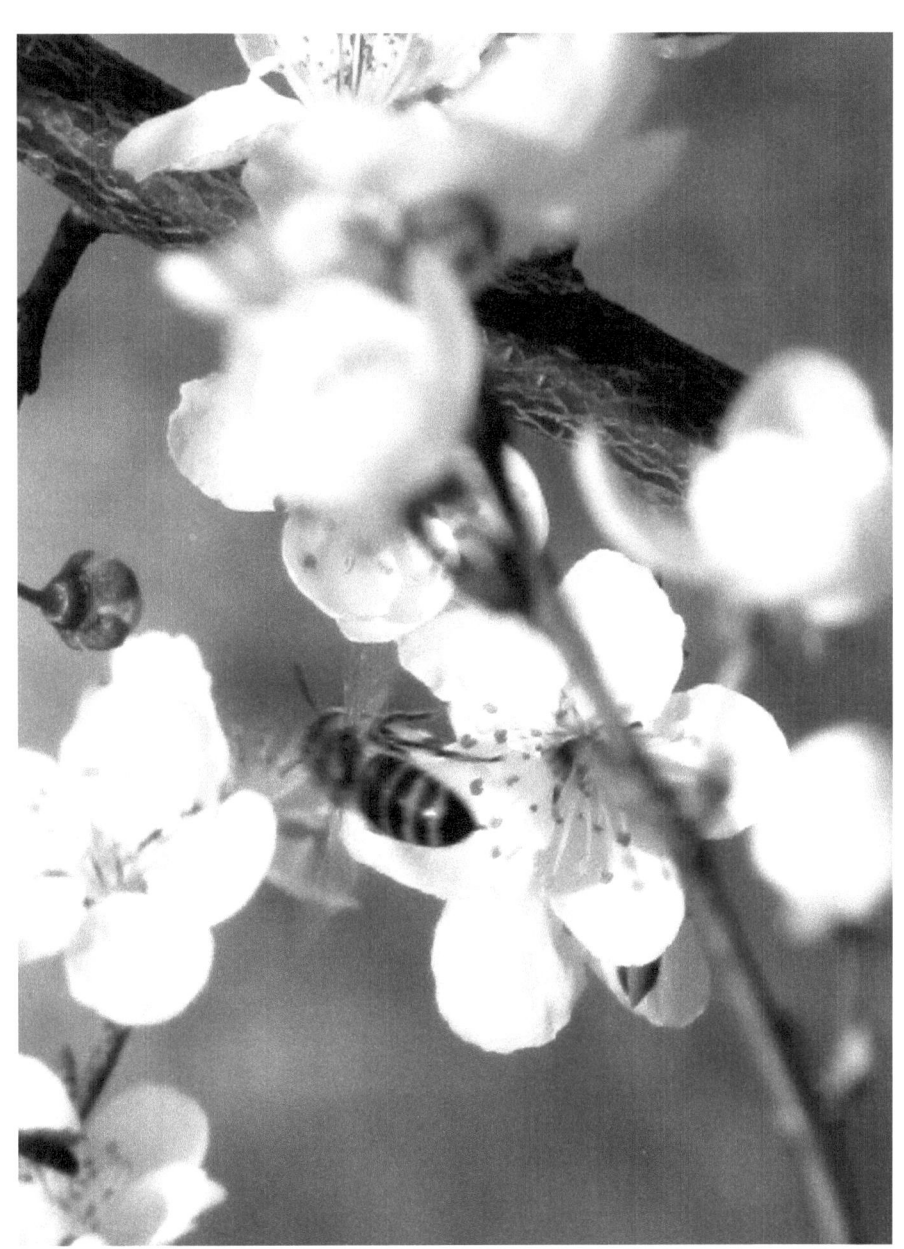

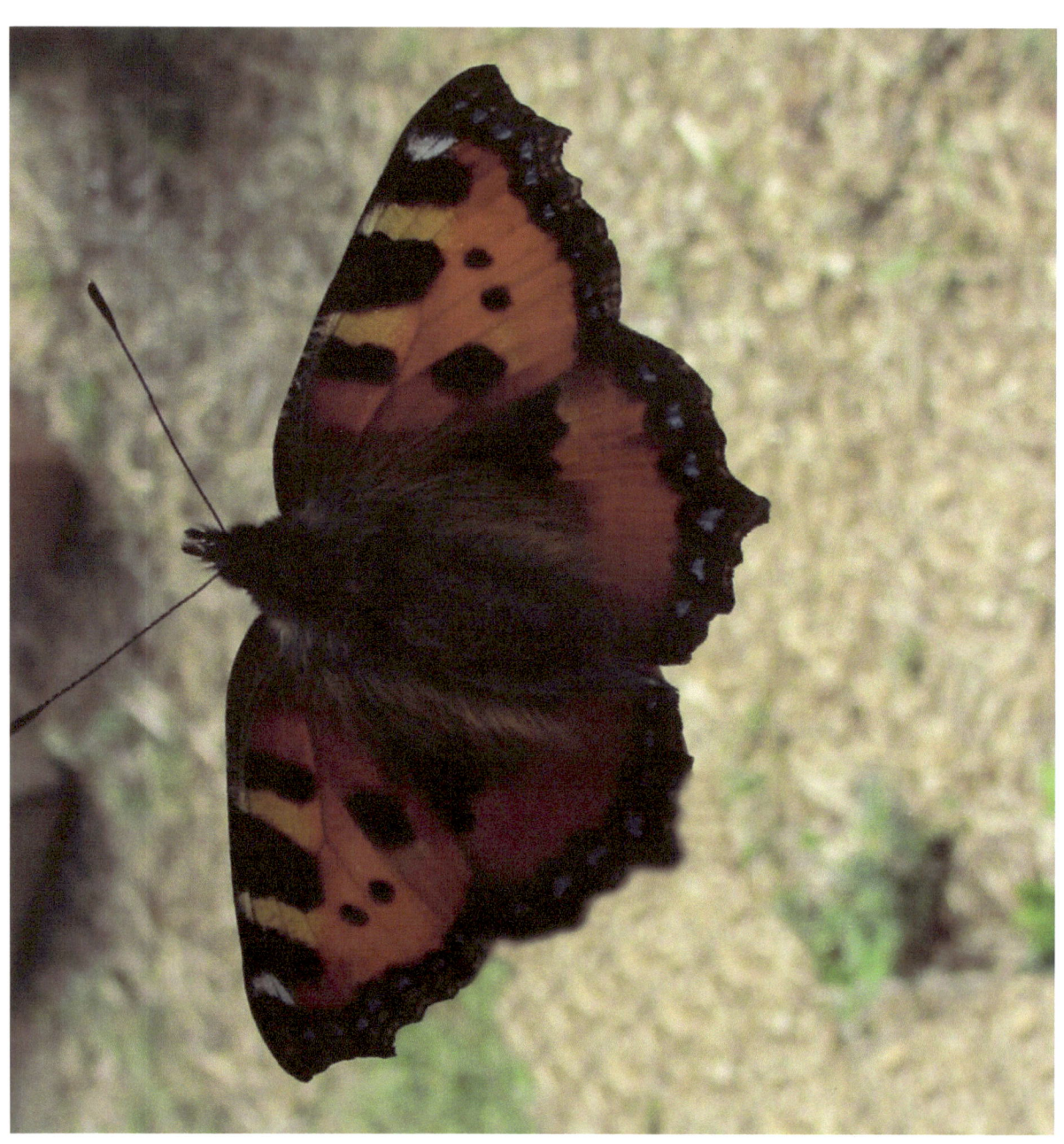

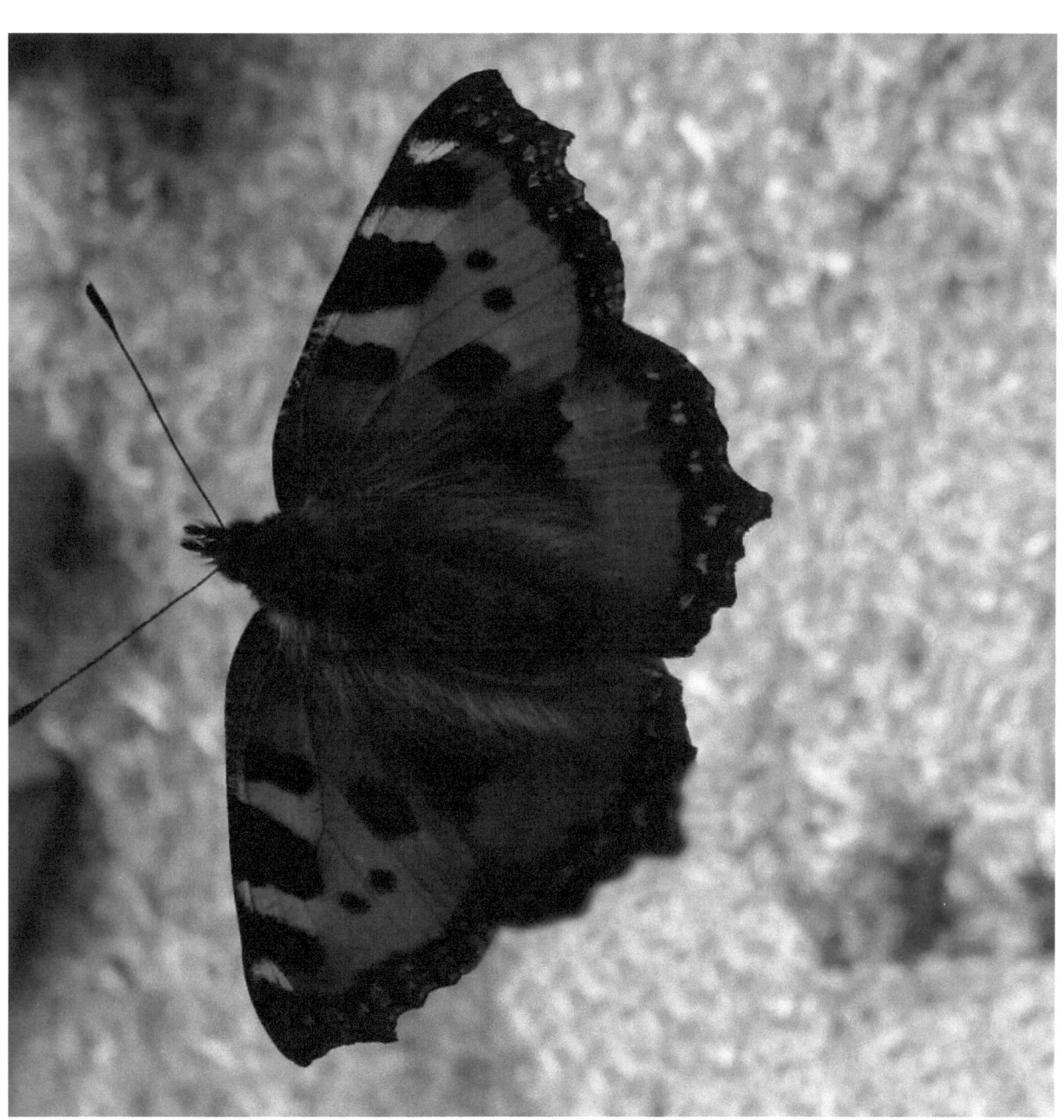

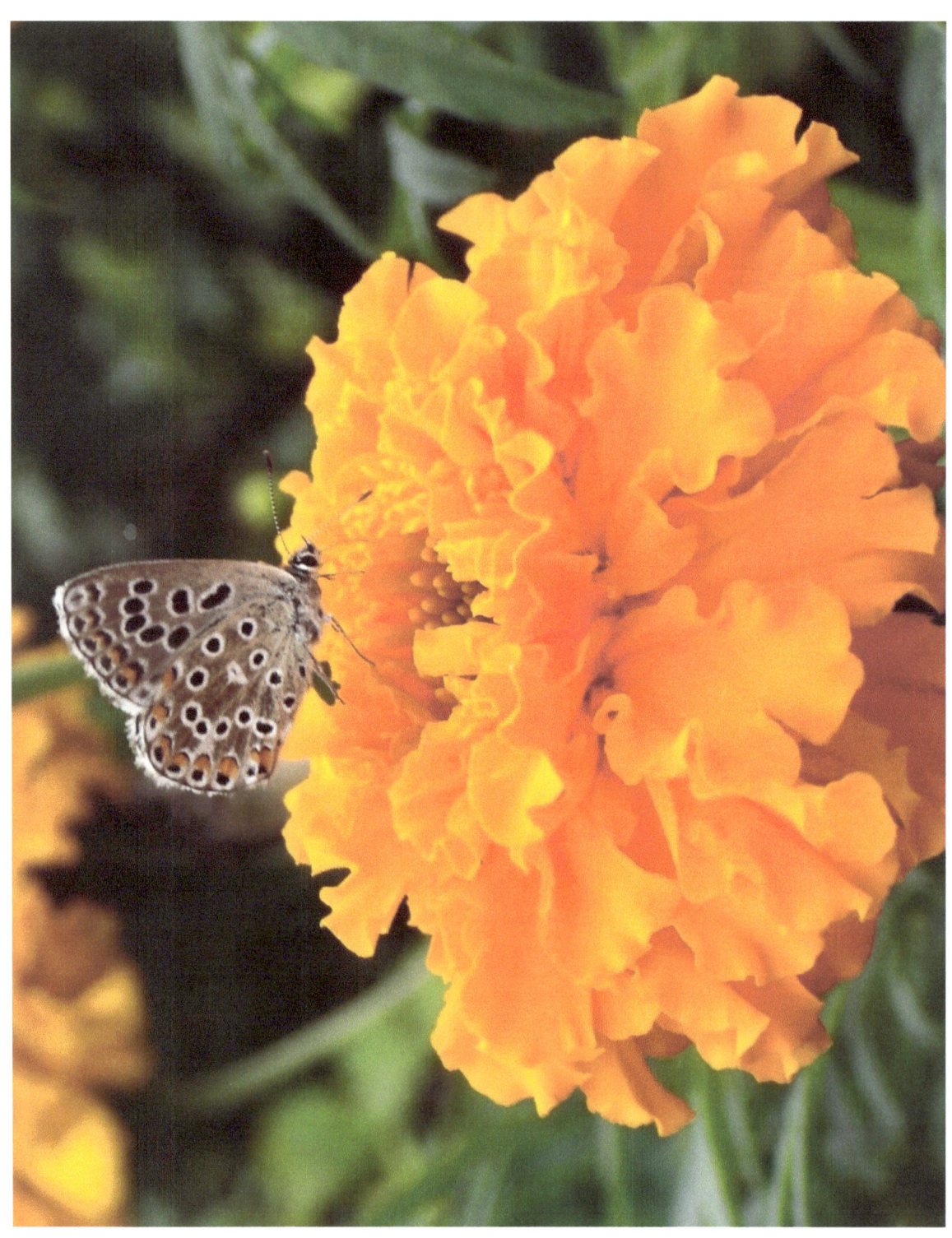

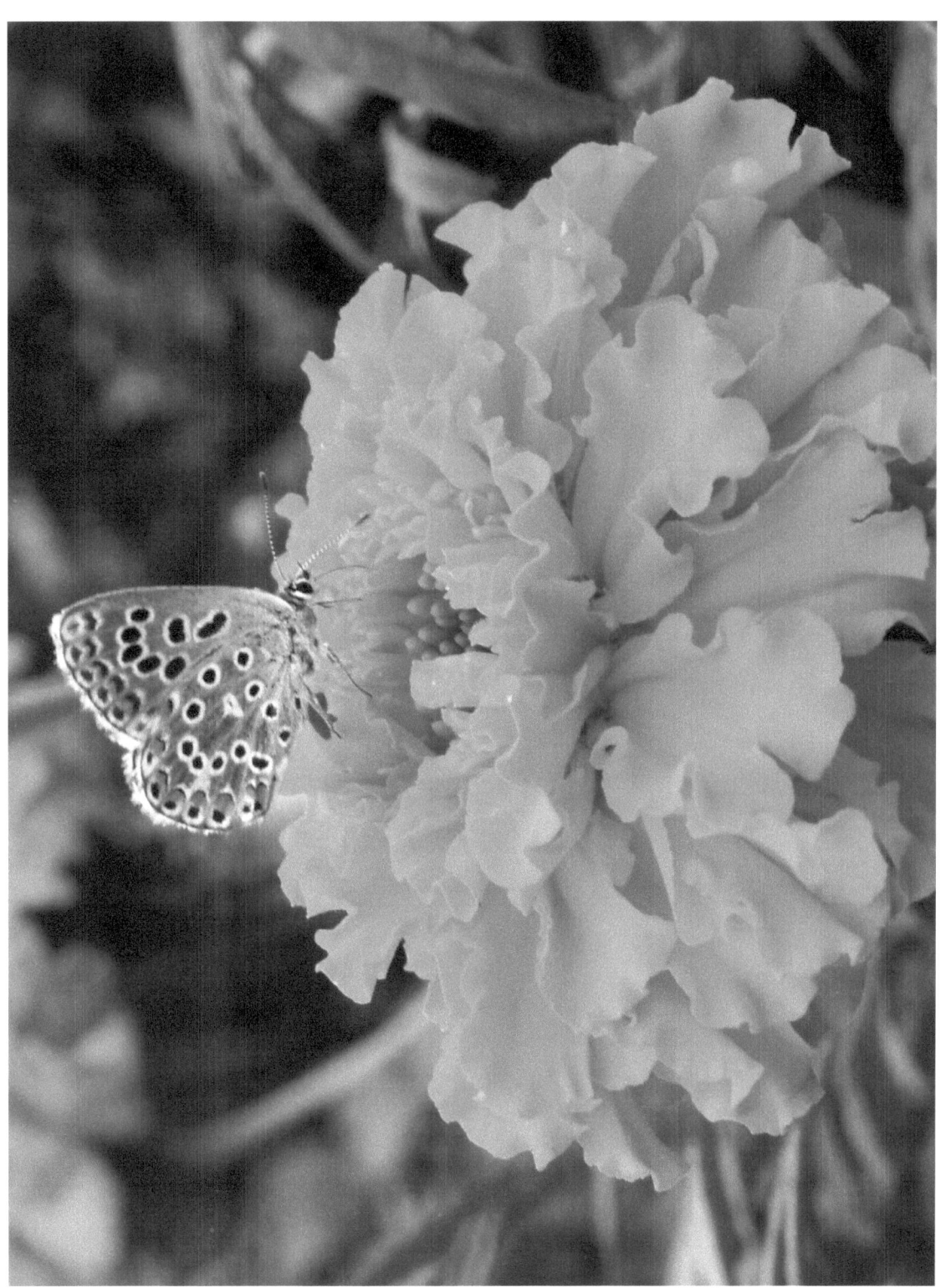

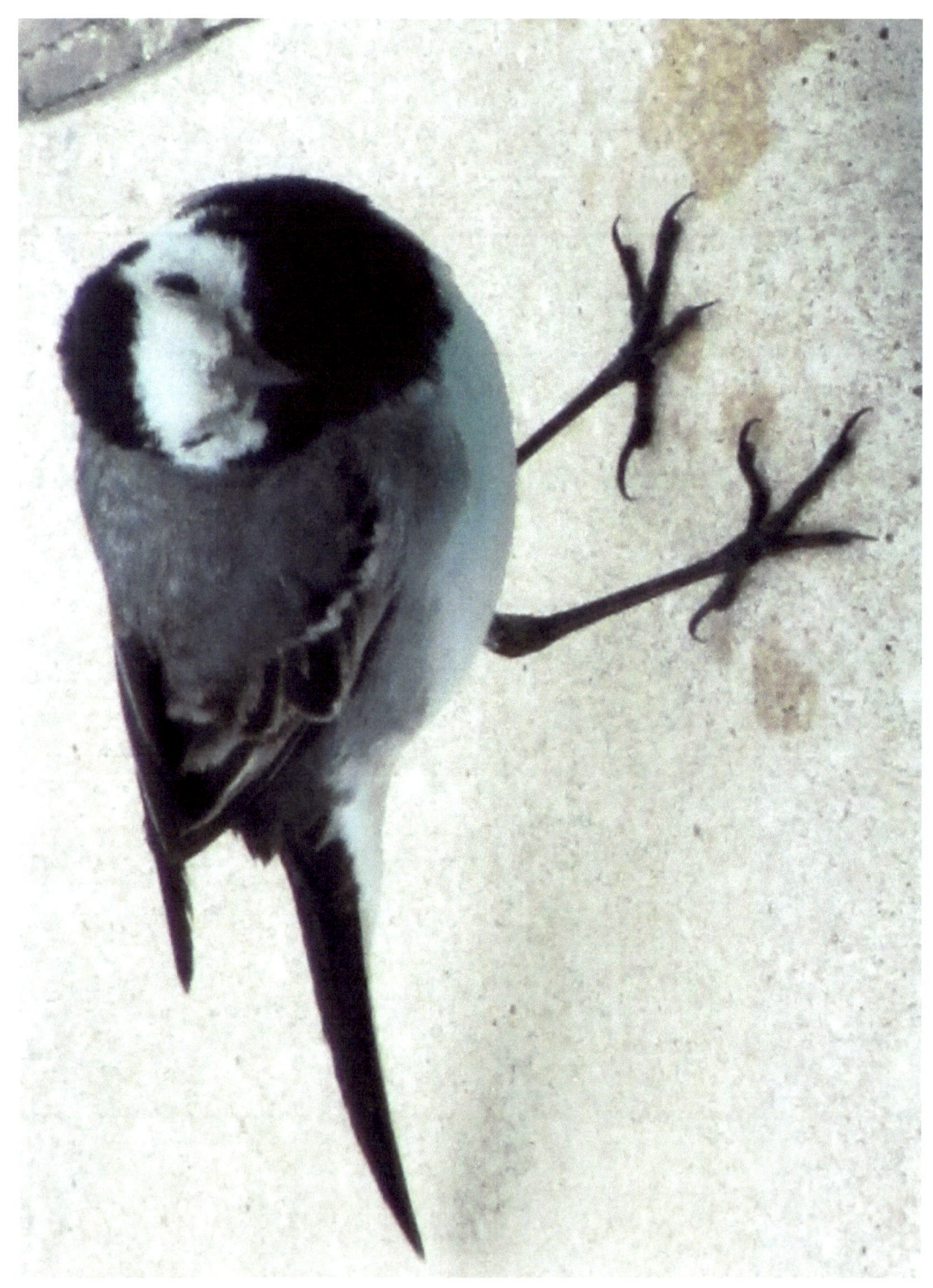

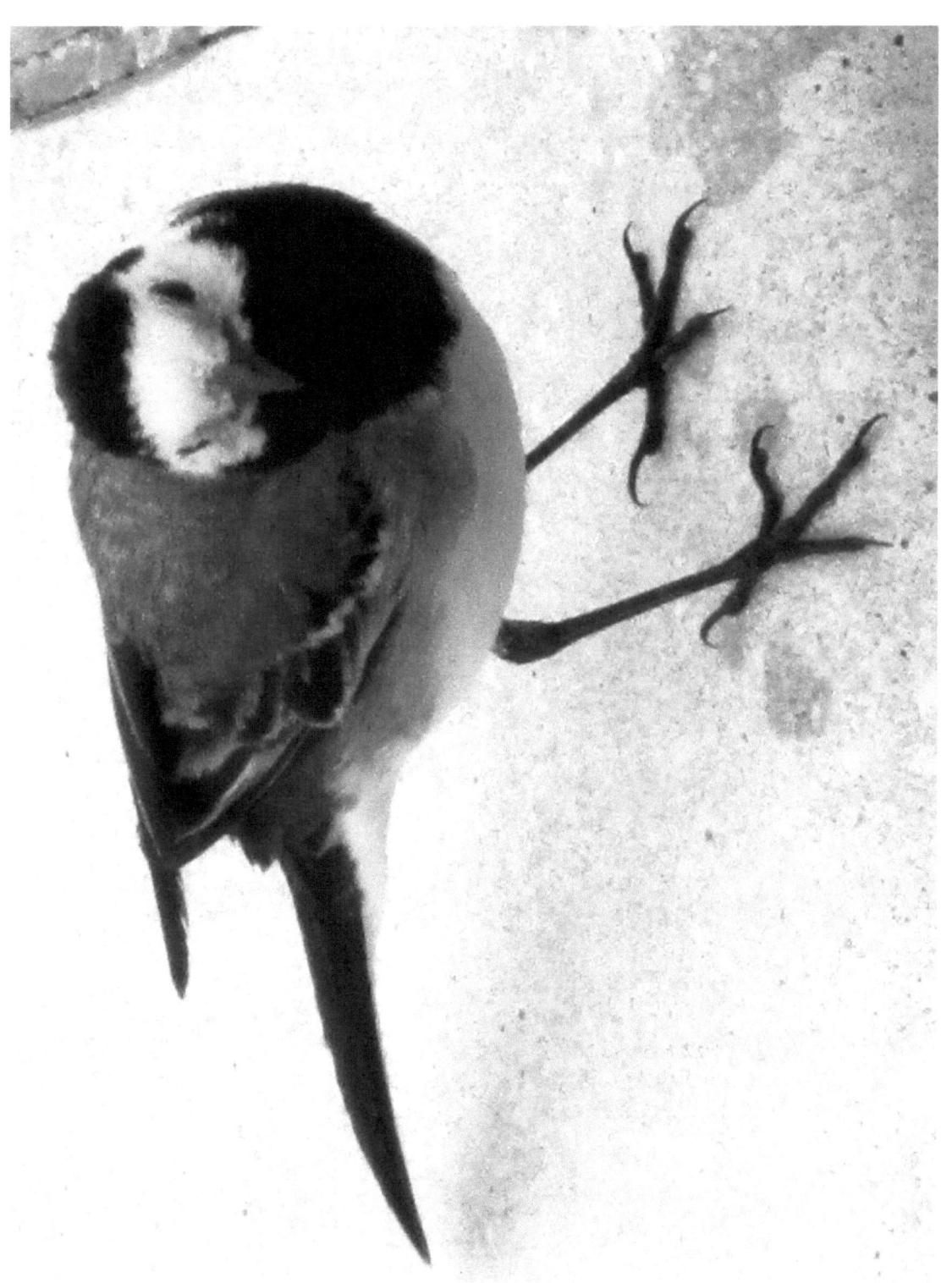

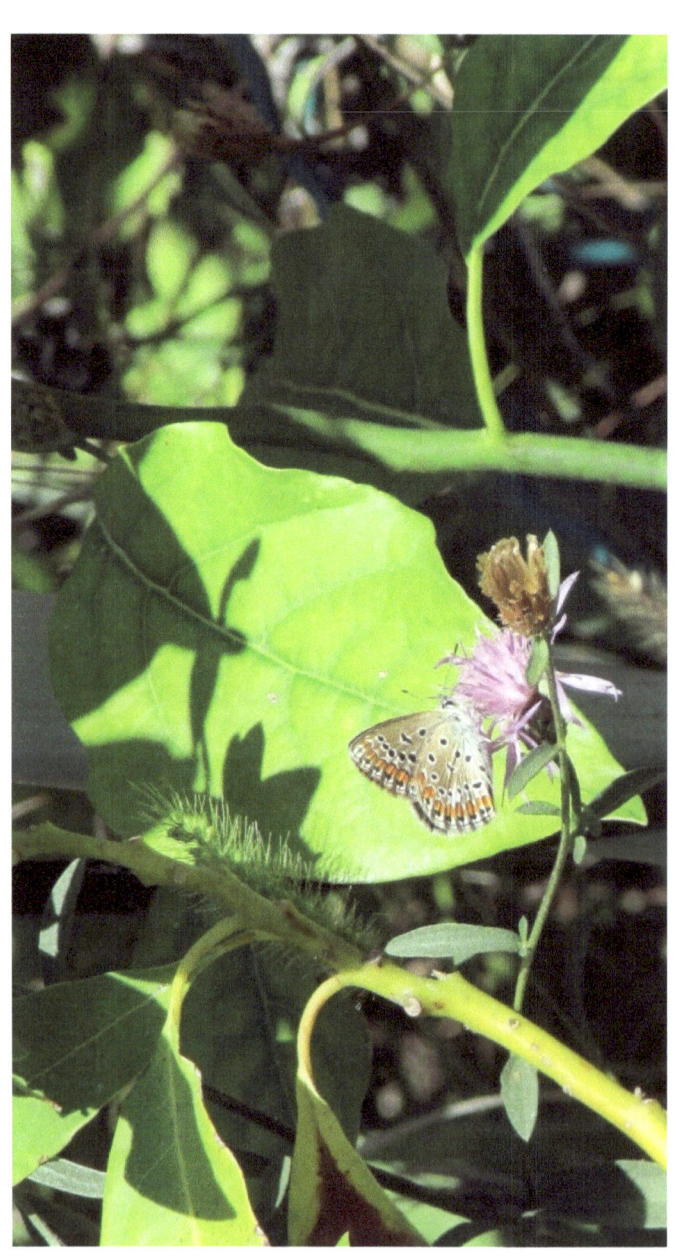

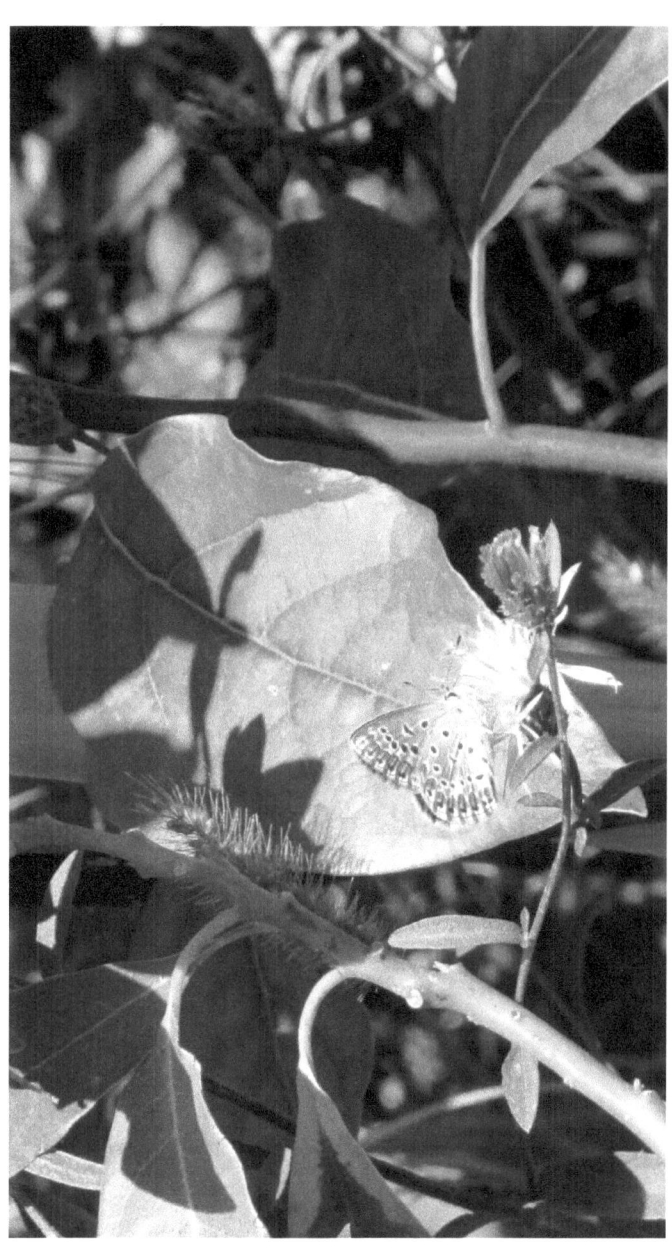

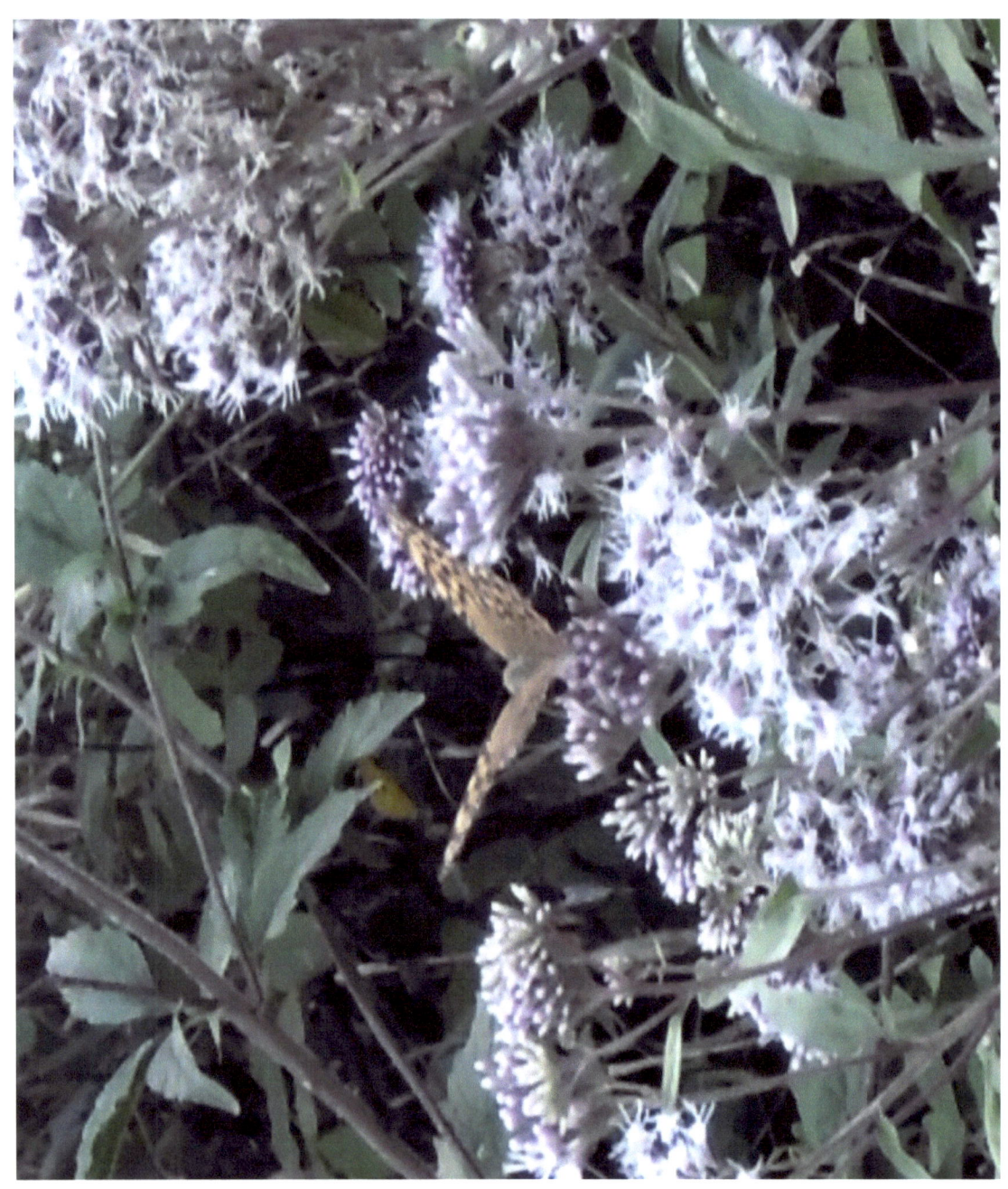

P 17

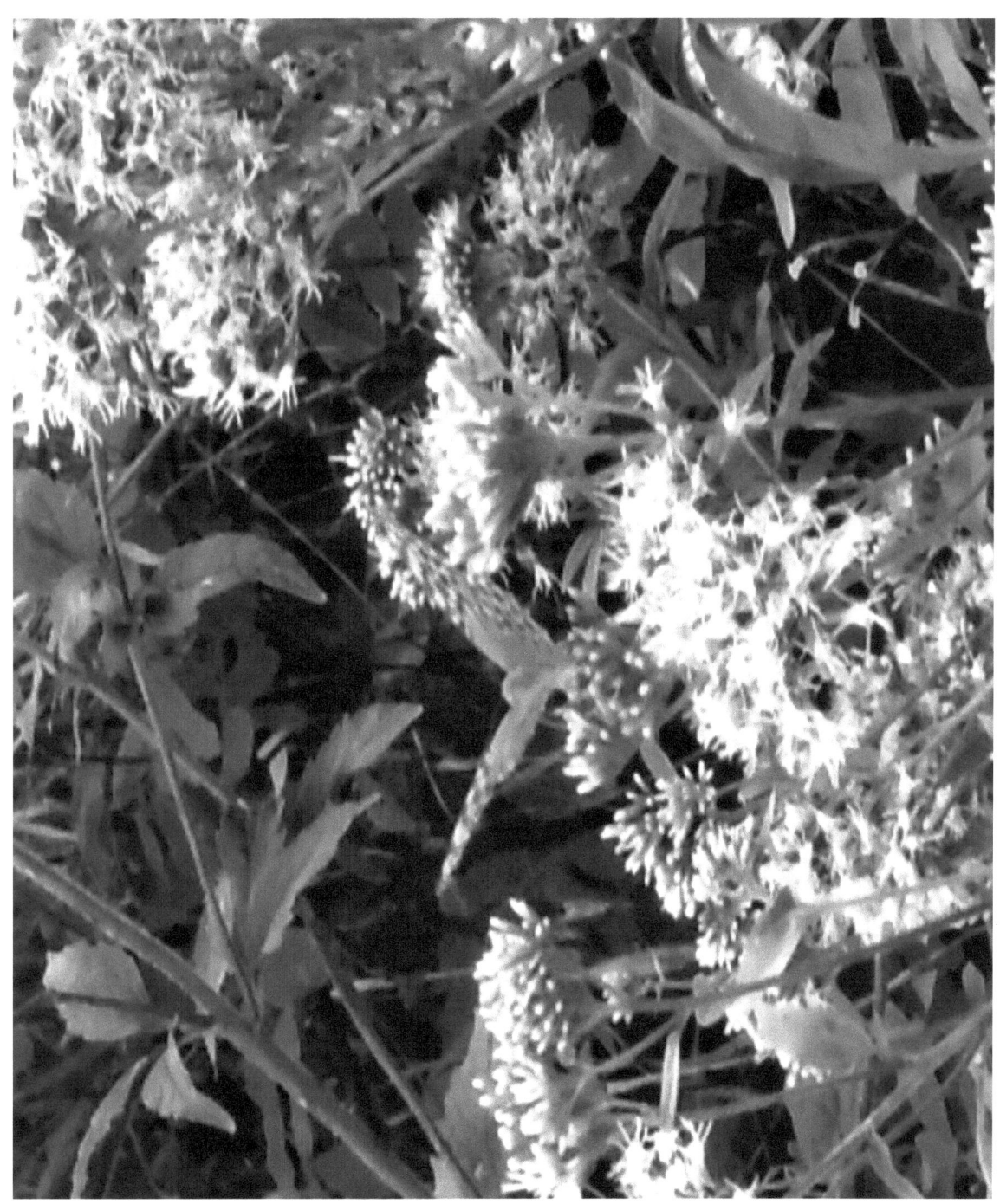

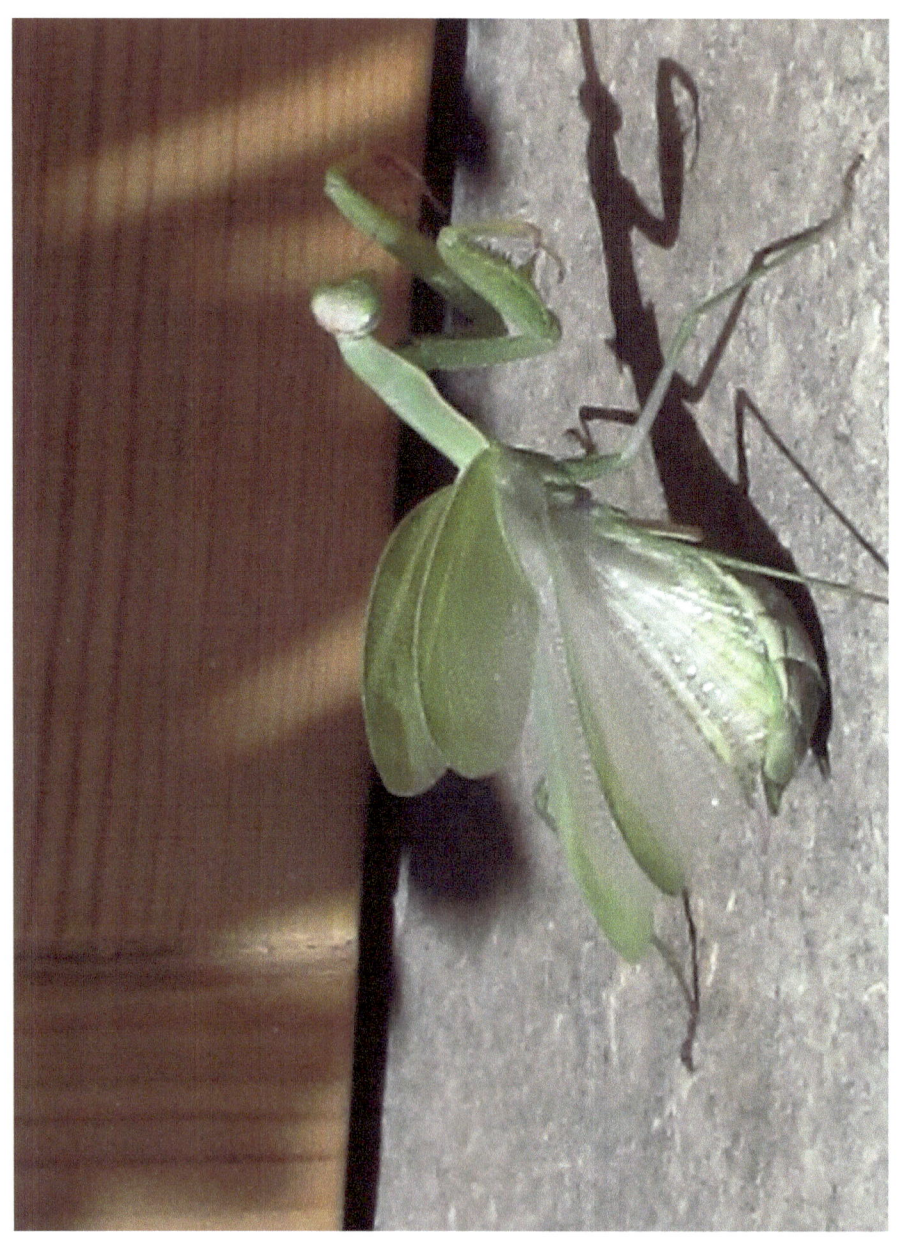

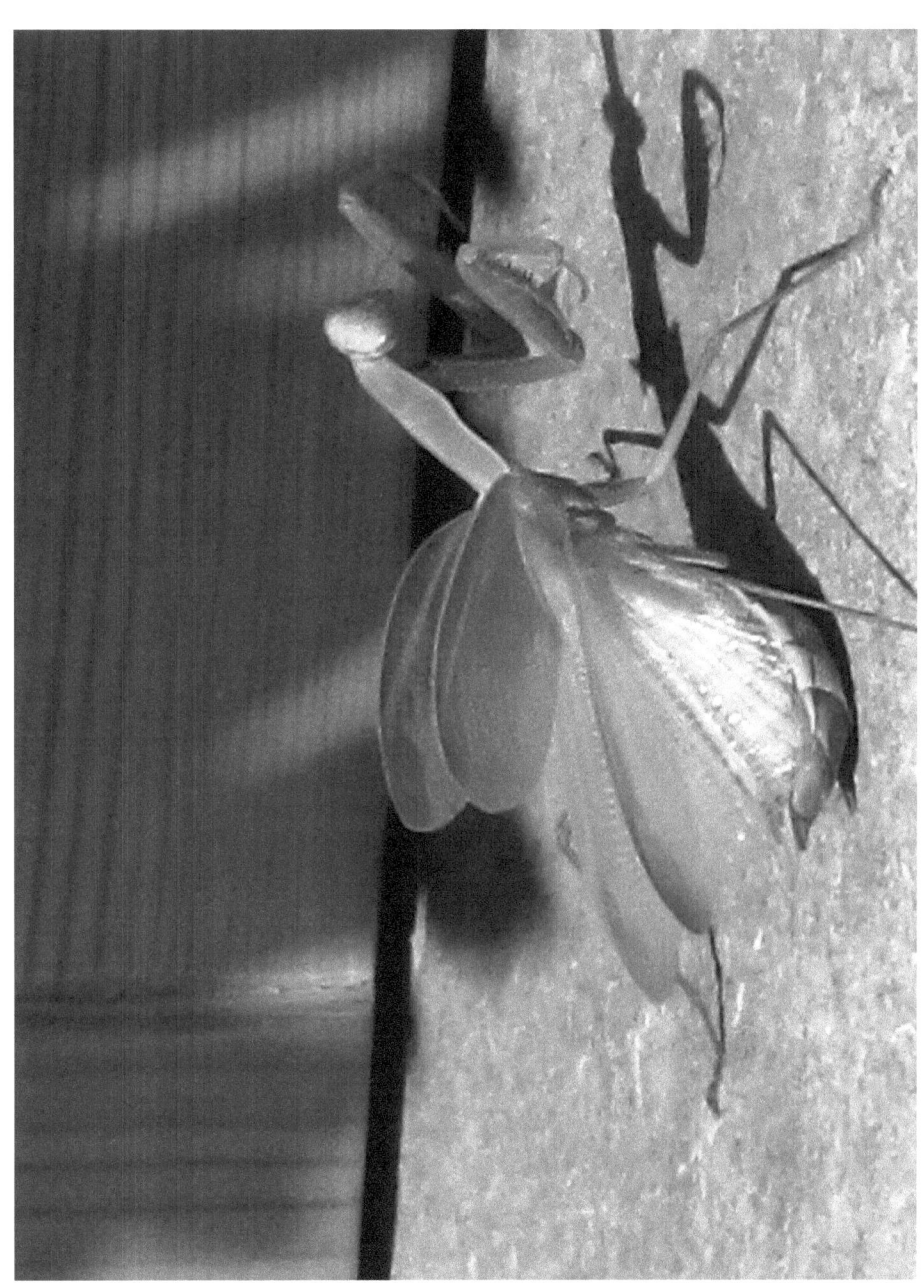

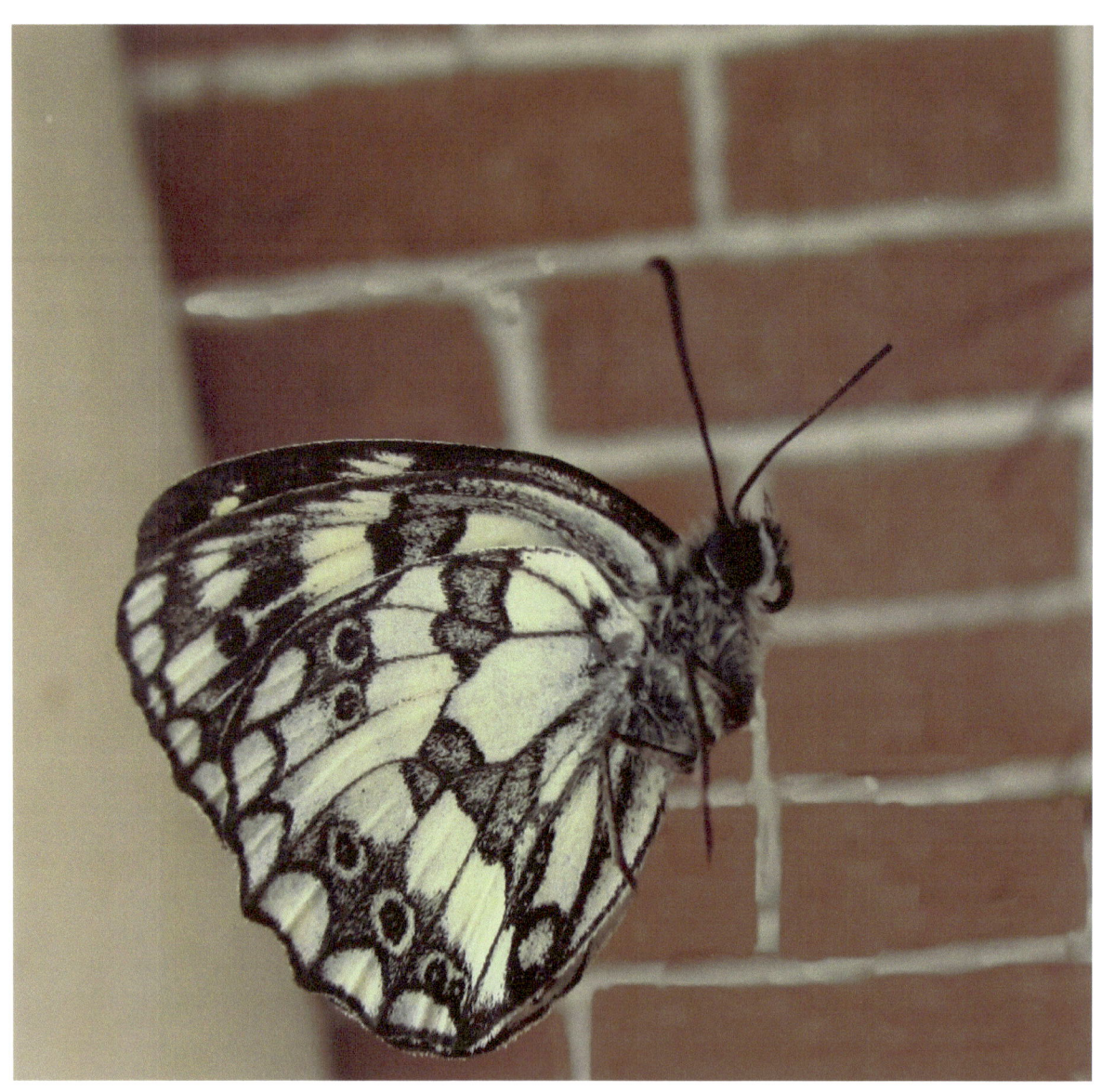

P 21

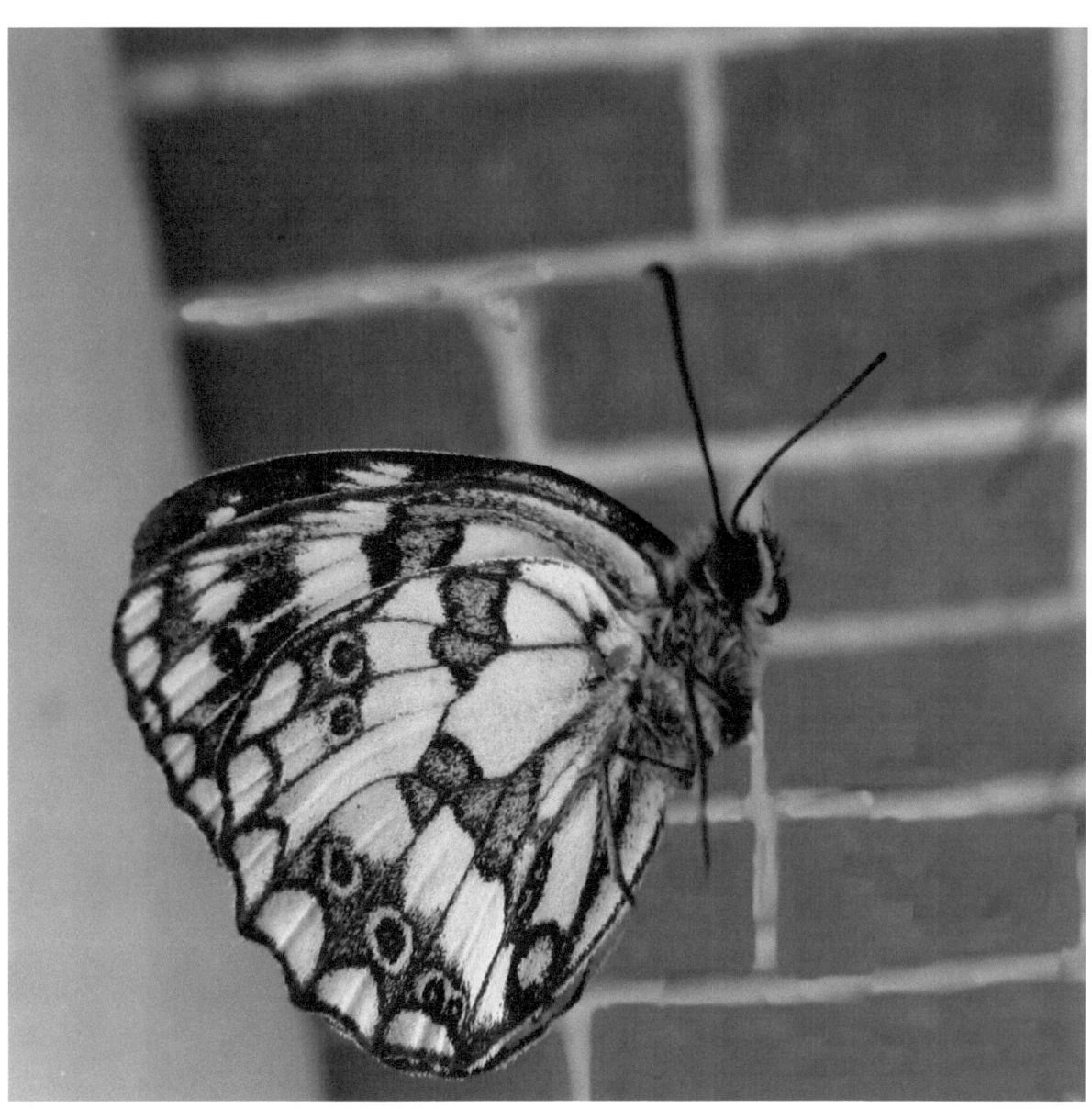

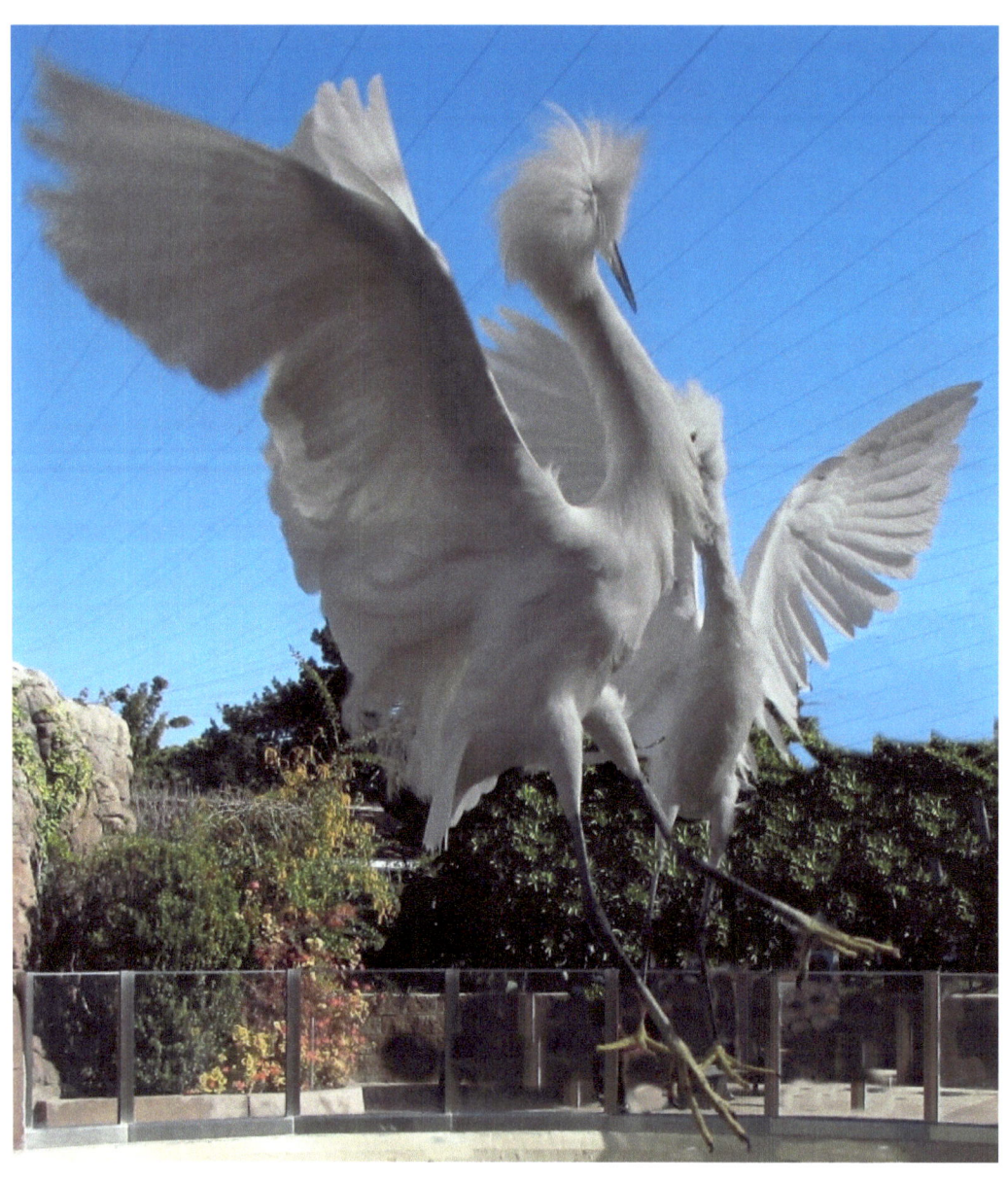

P 23

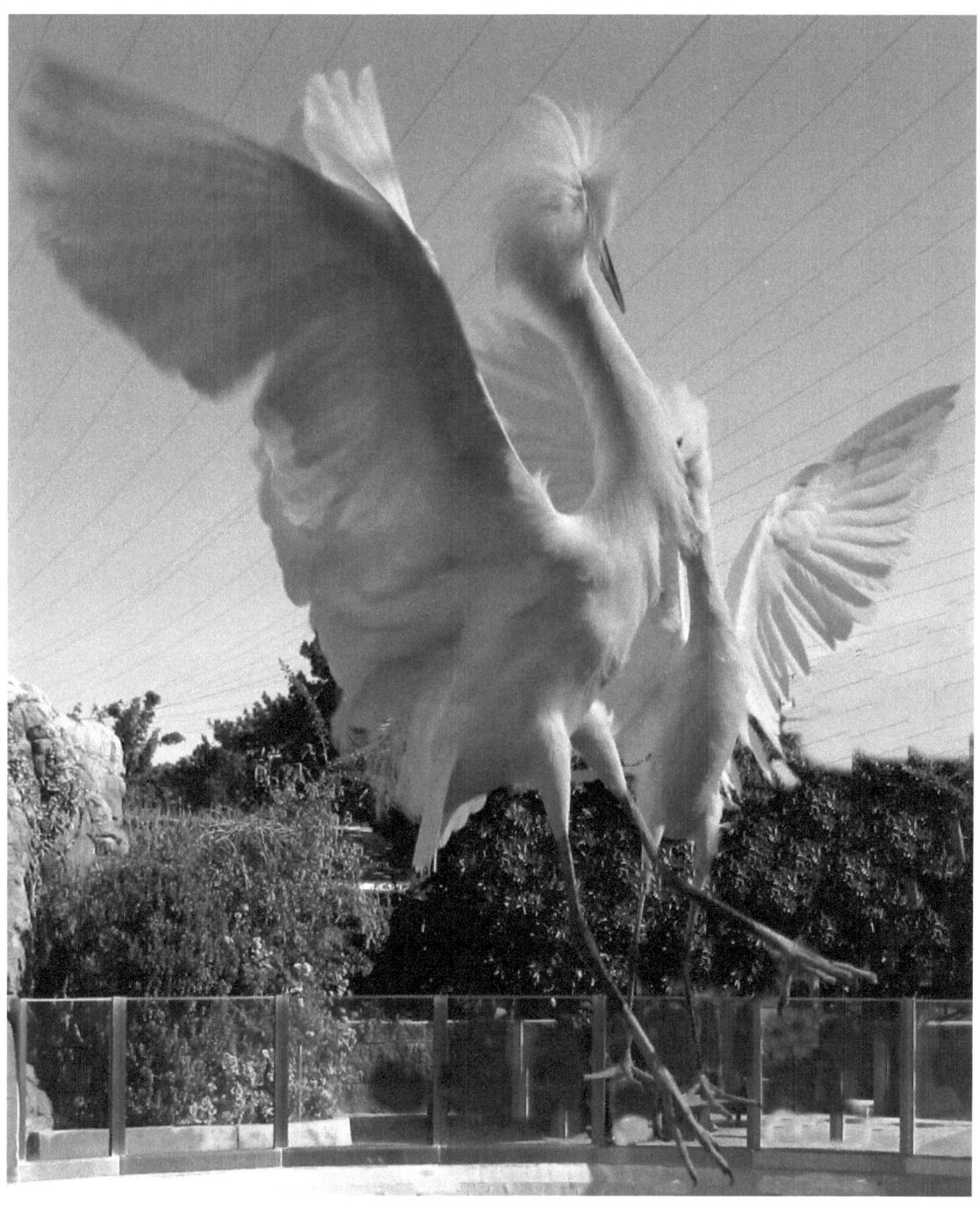

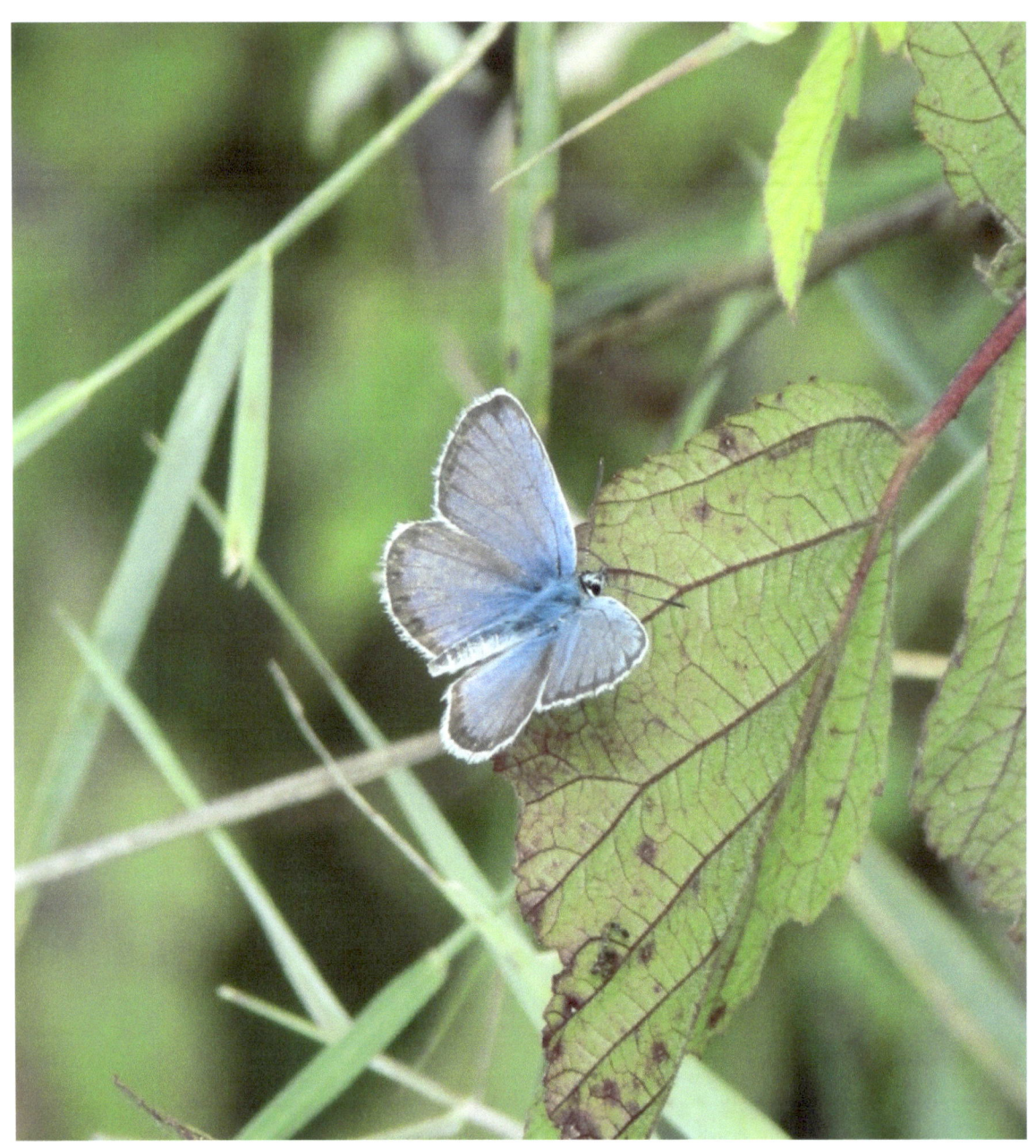

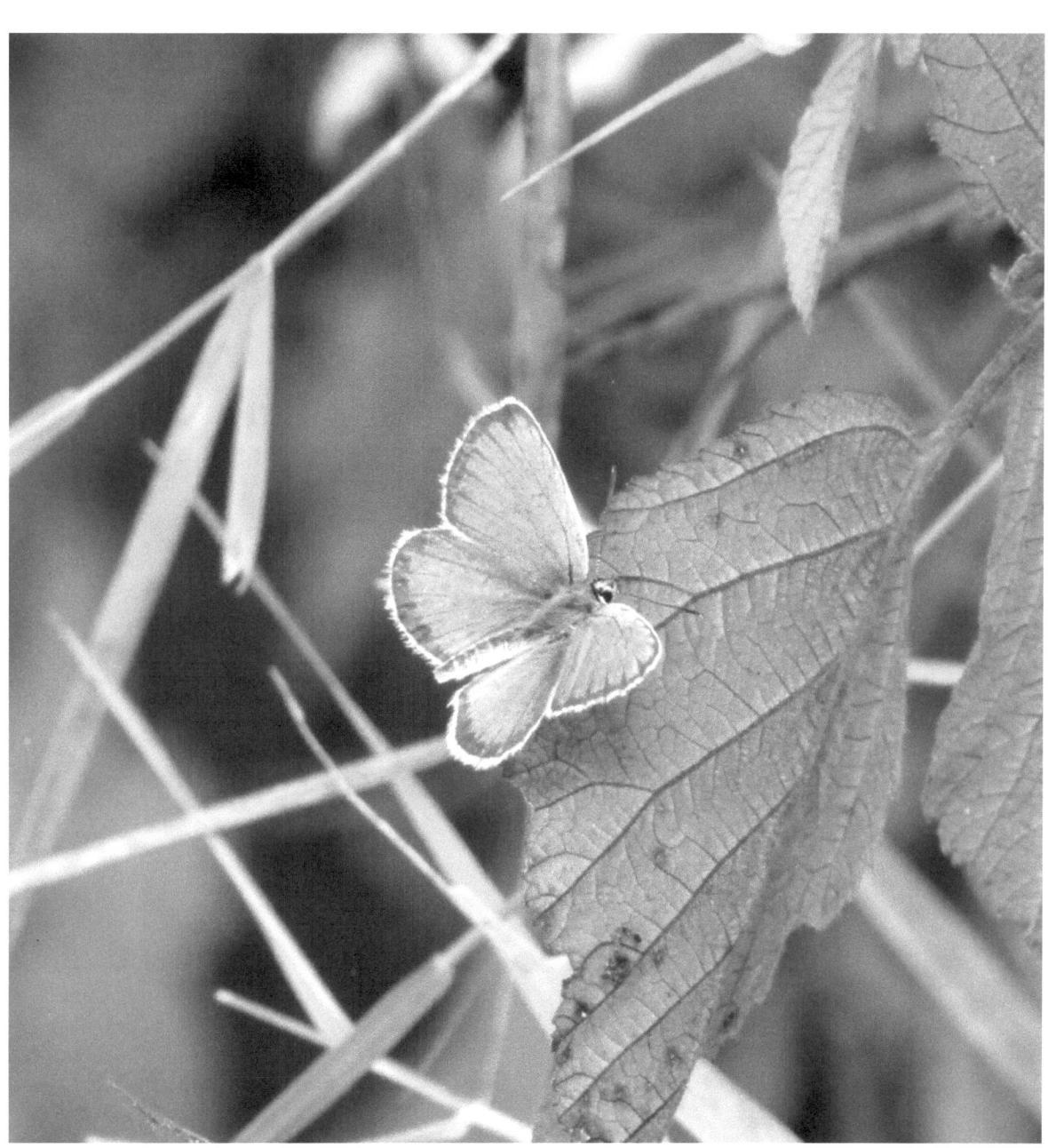

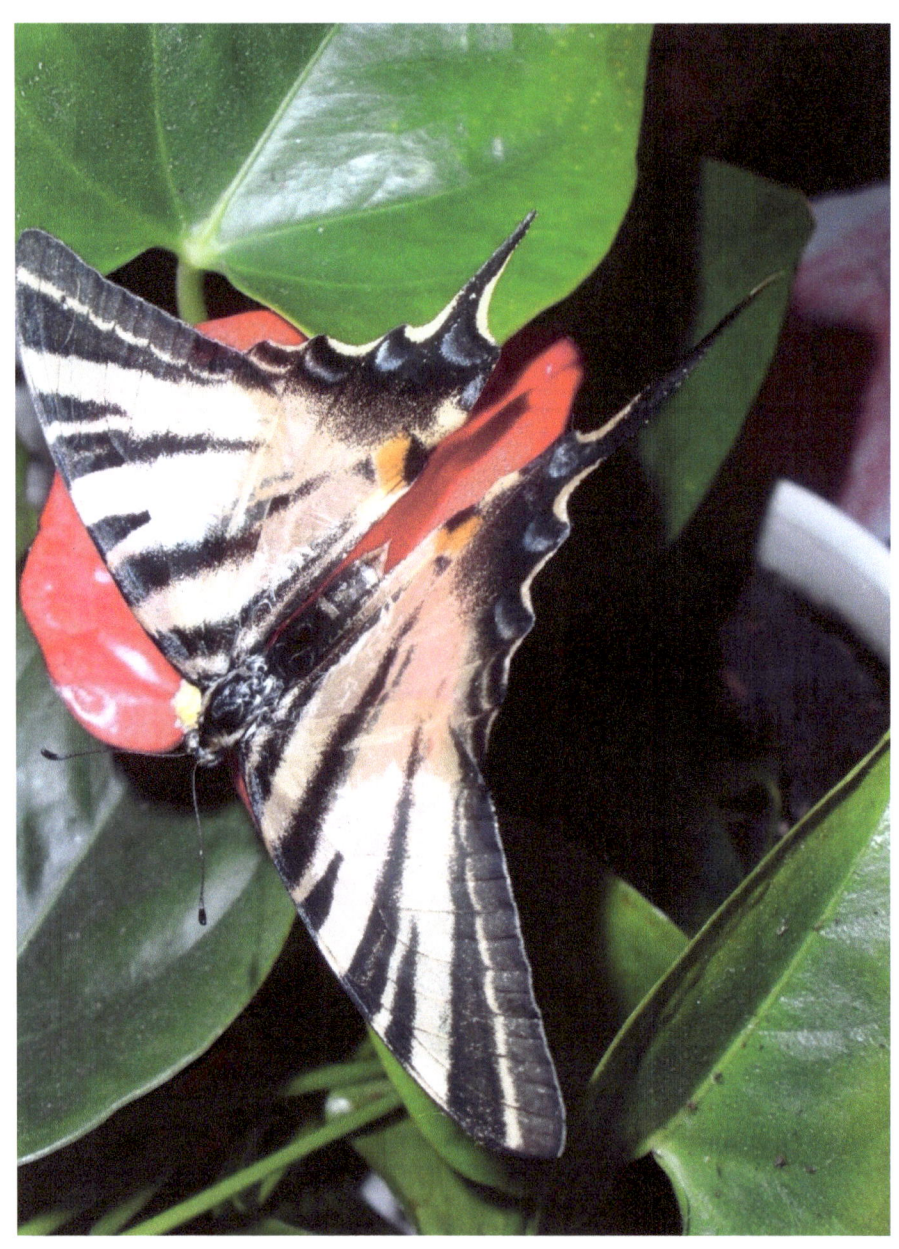

P 27

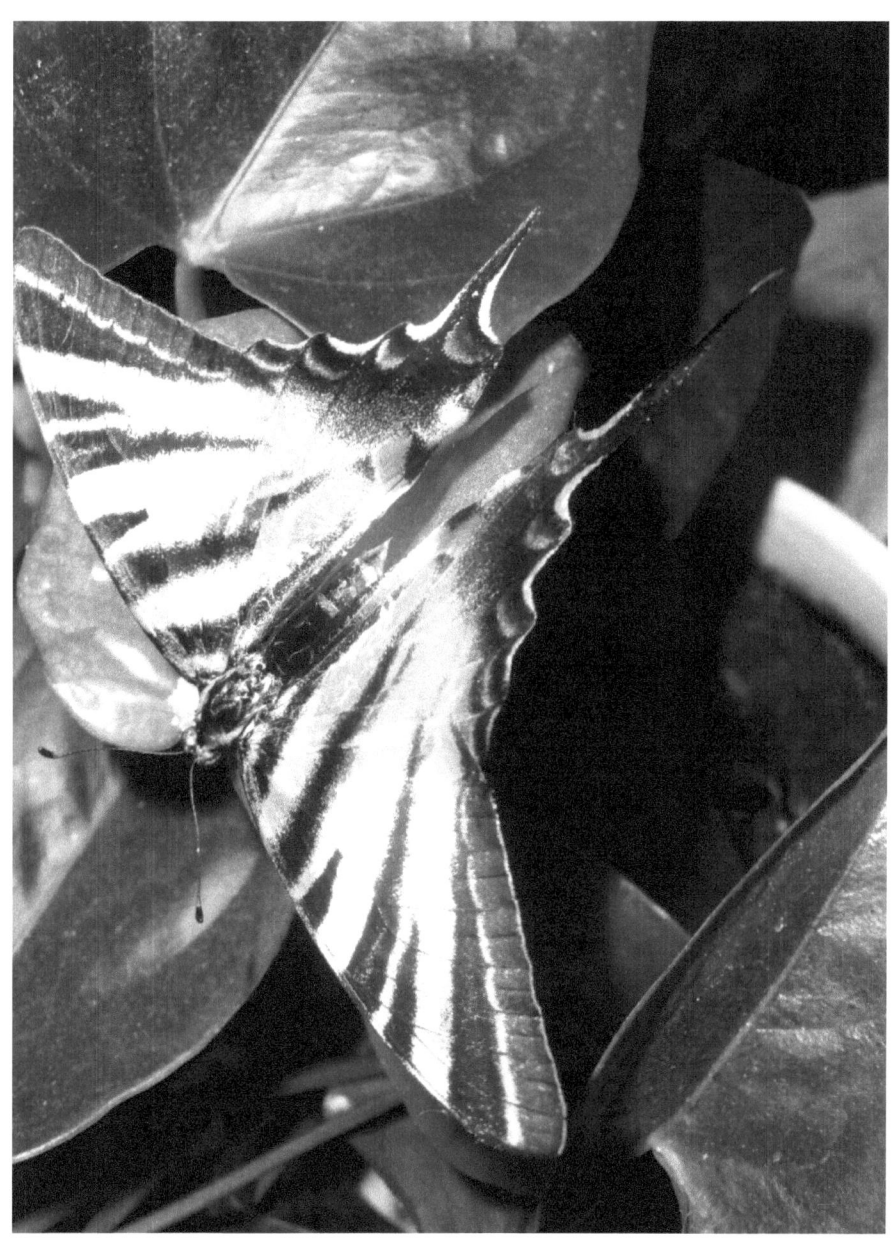

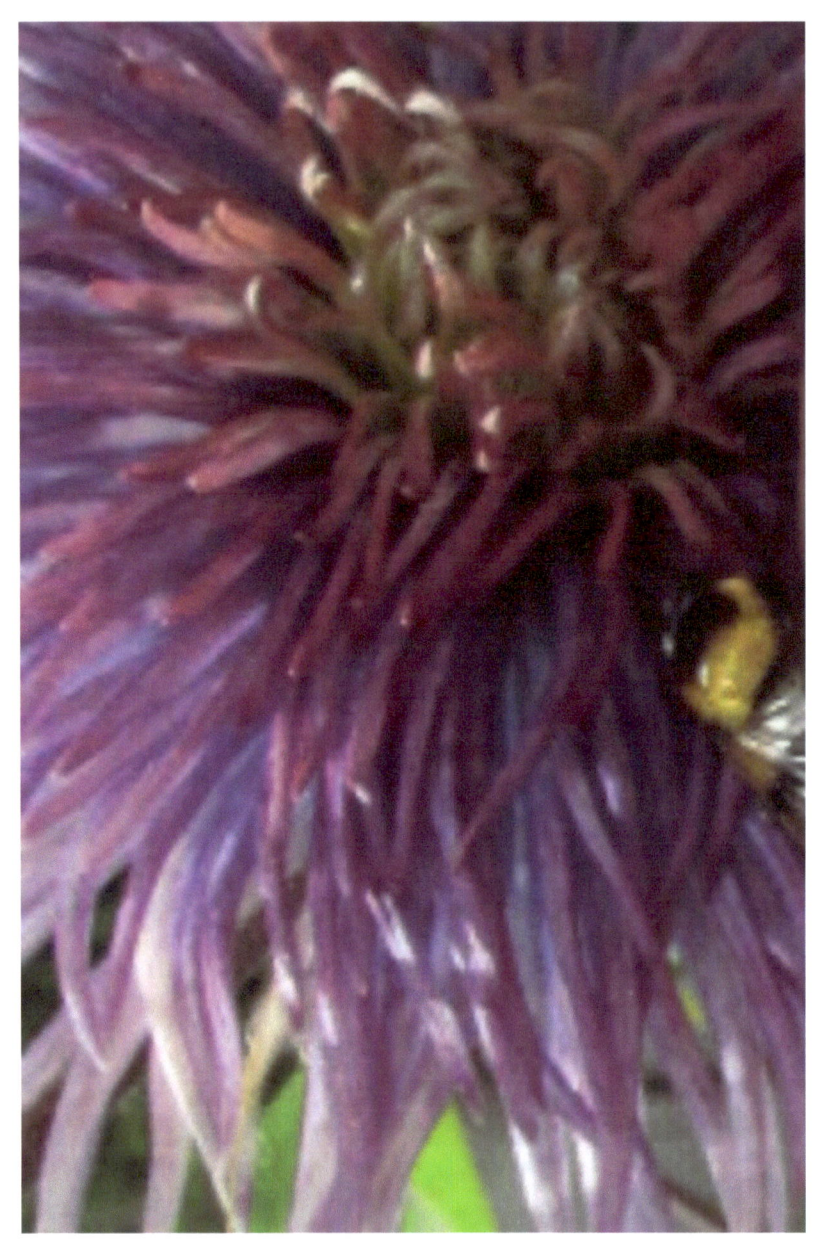

P 29

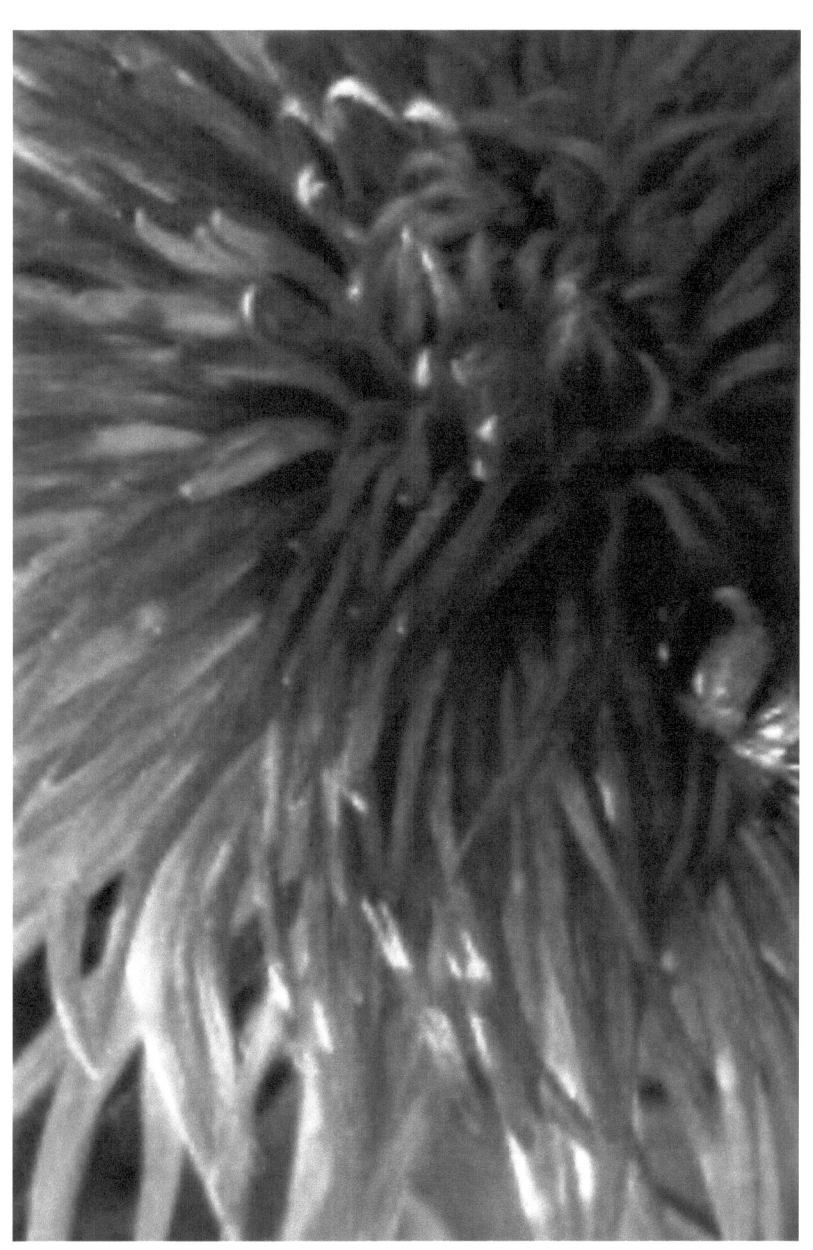

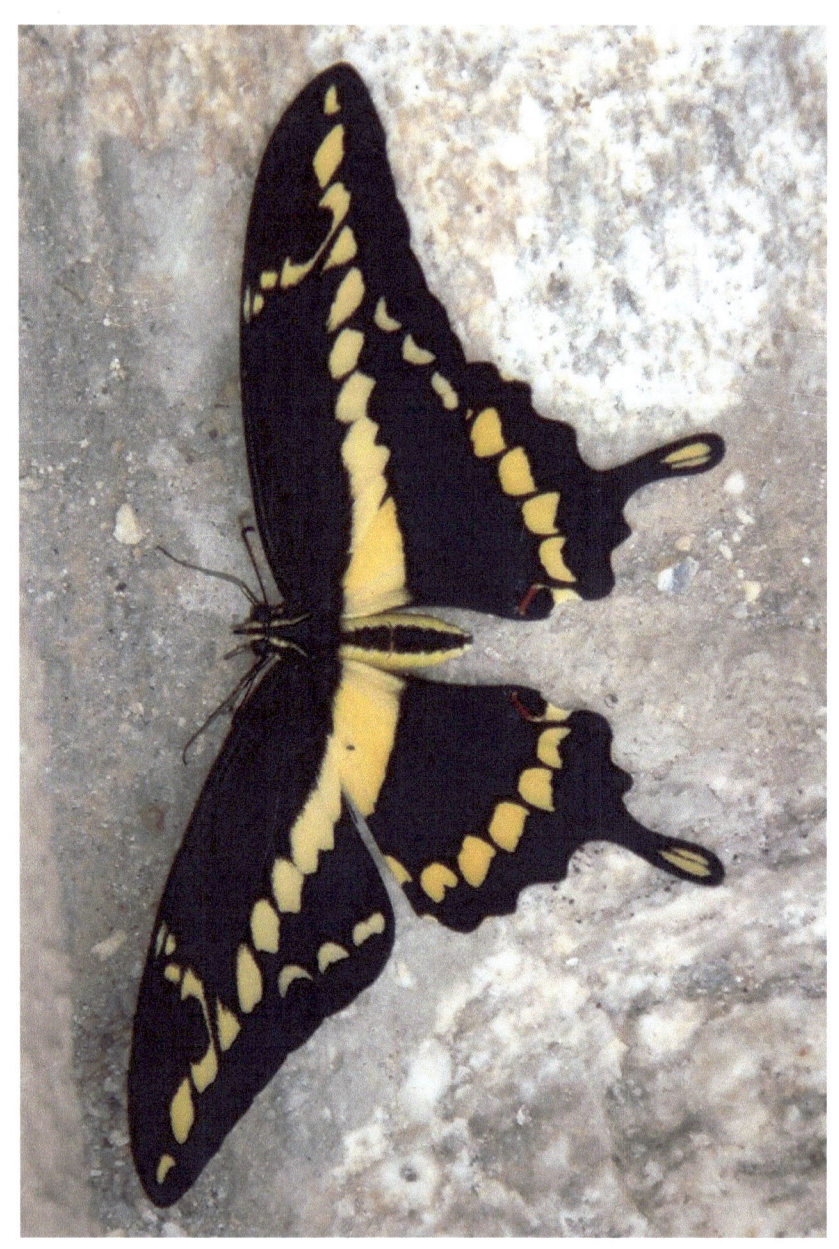

P 31

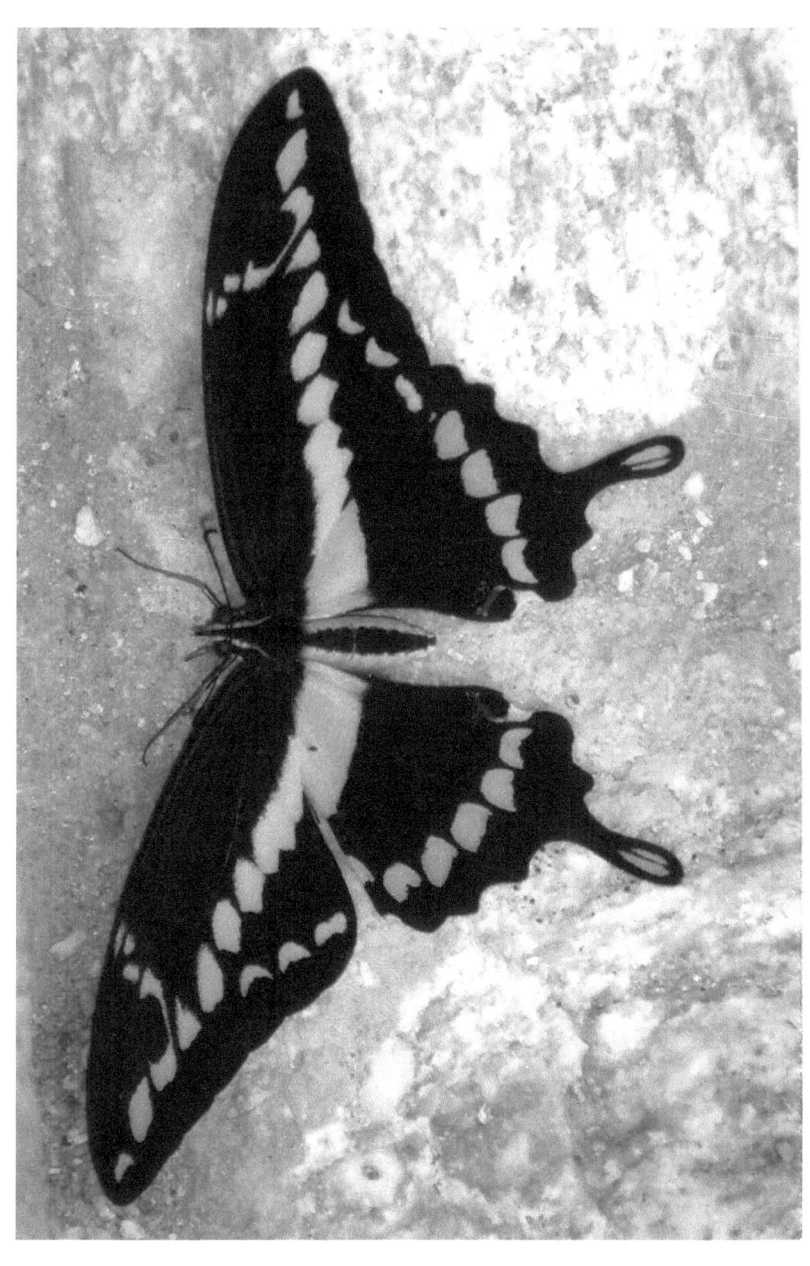

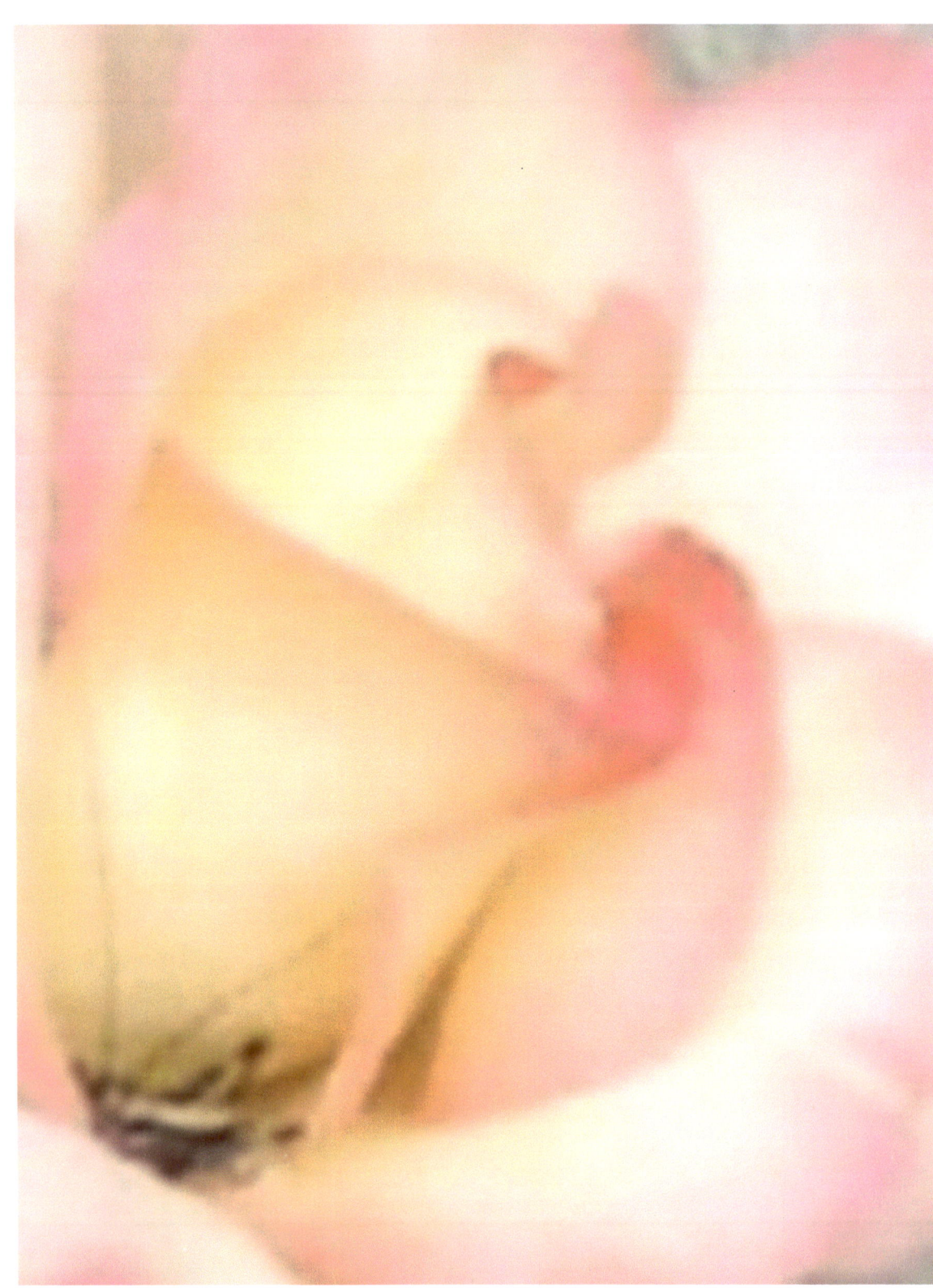

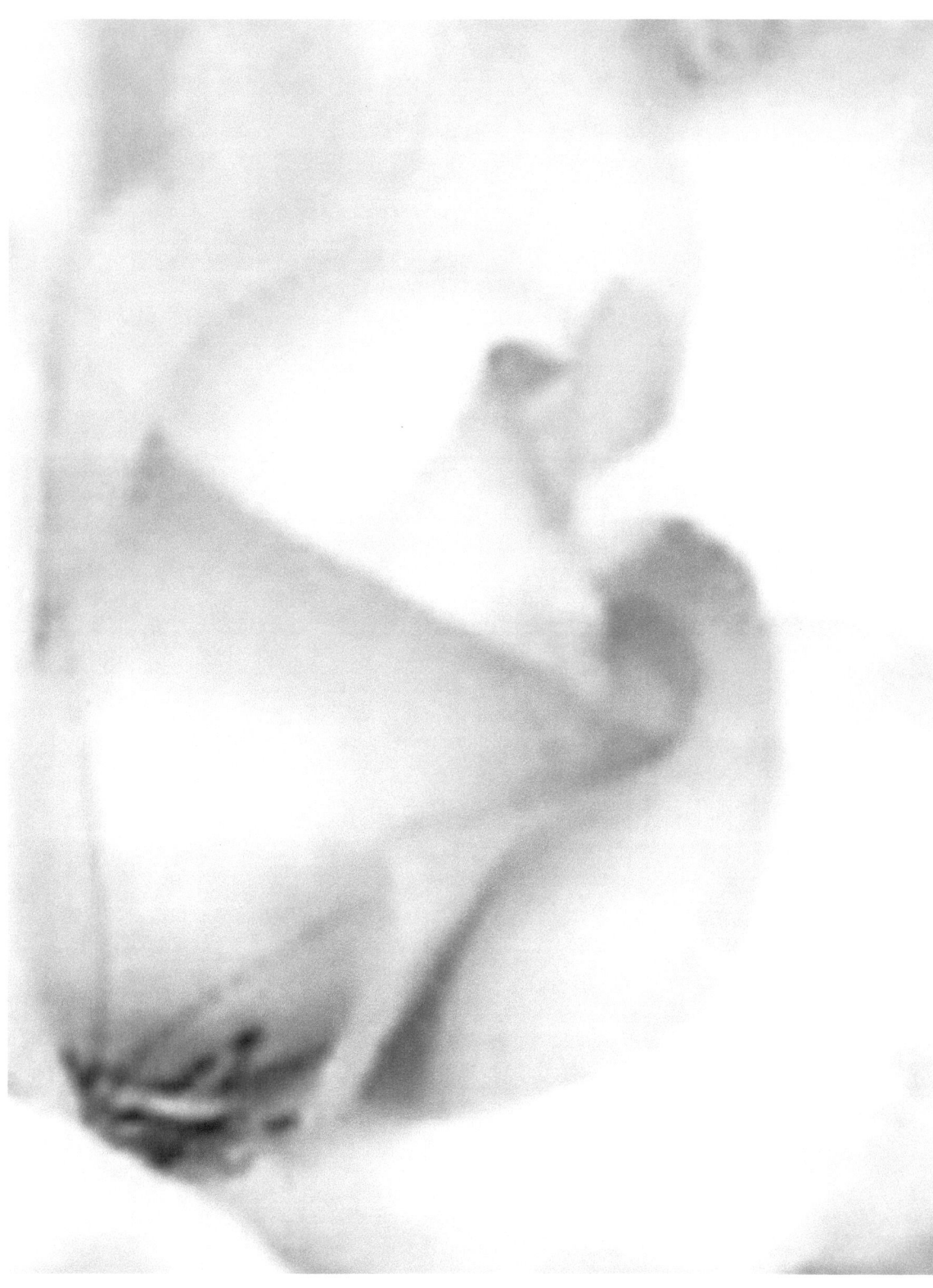

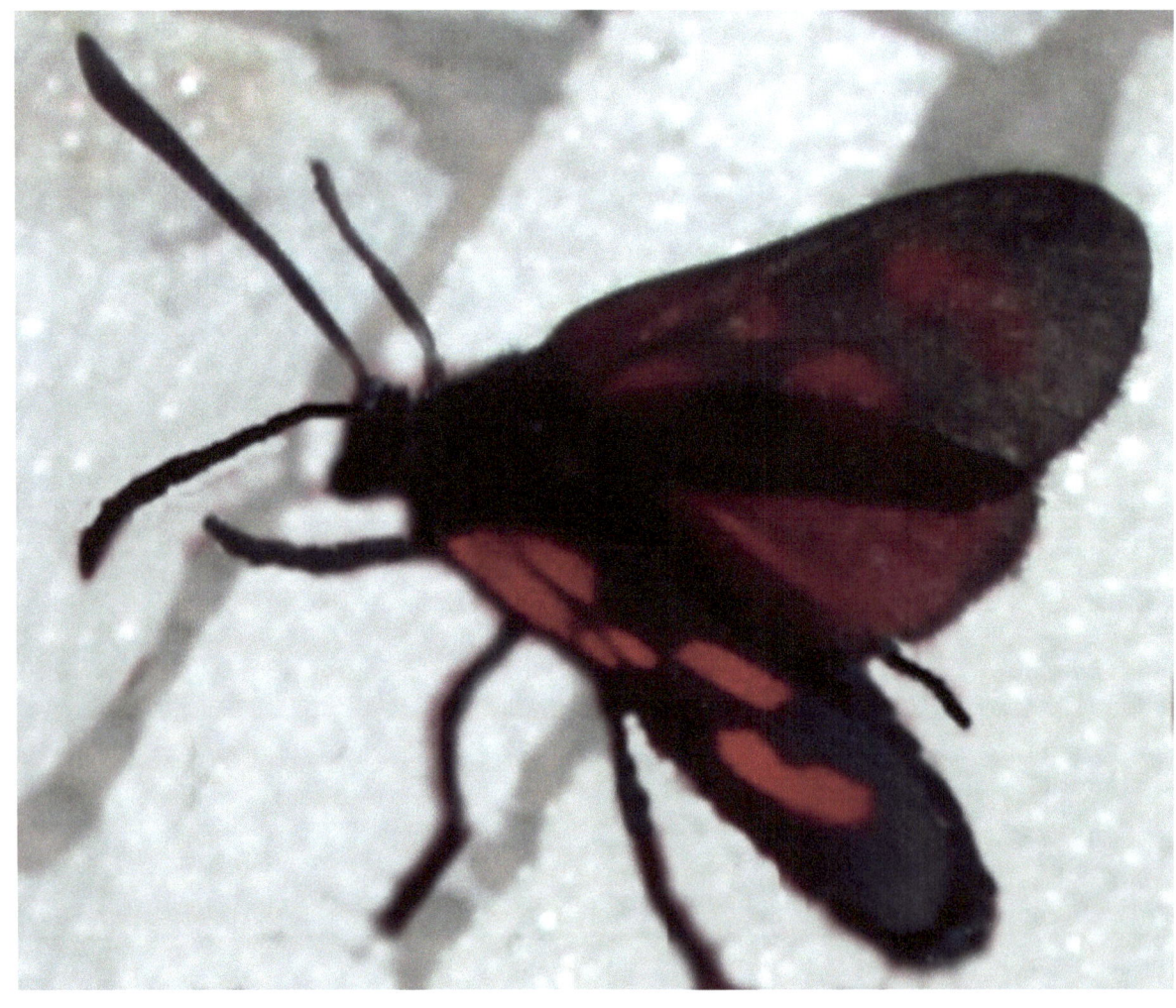

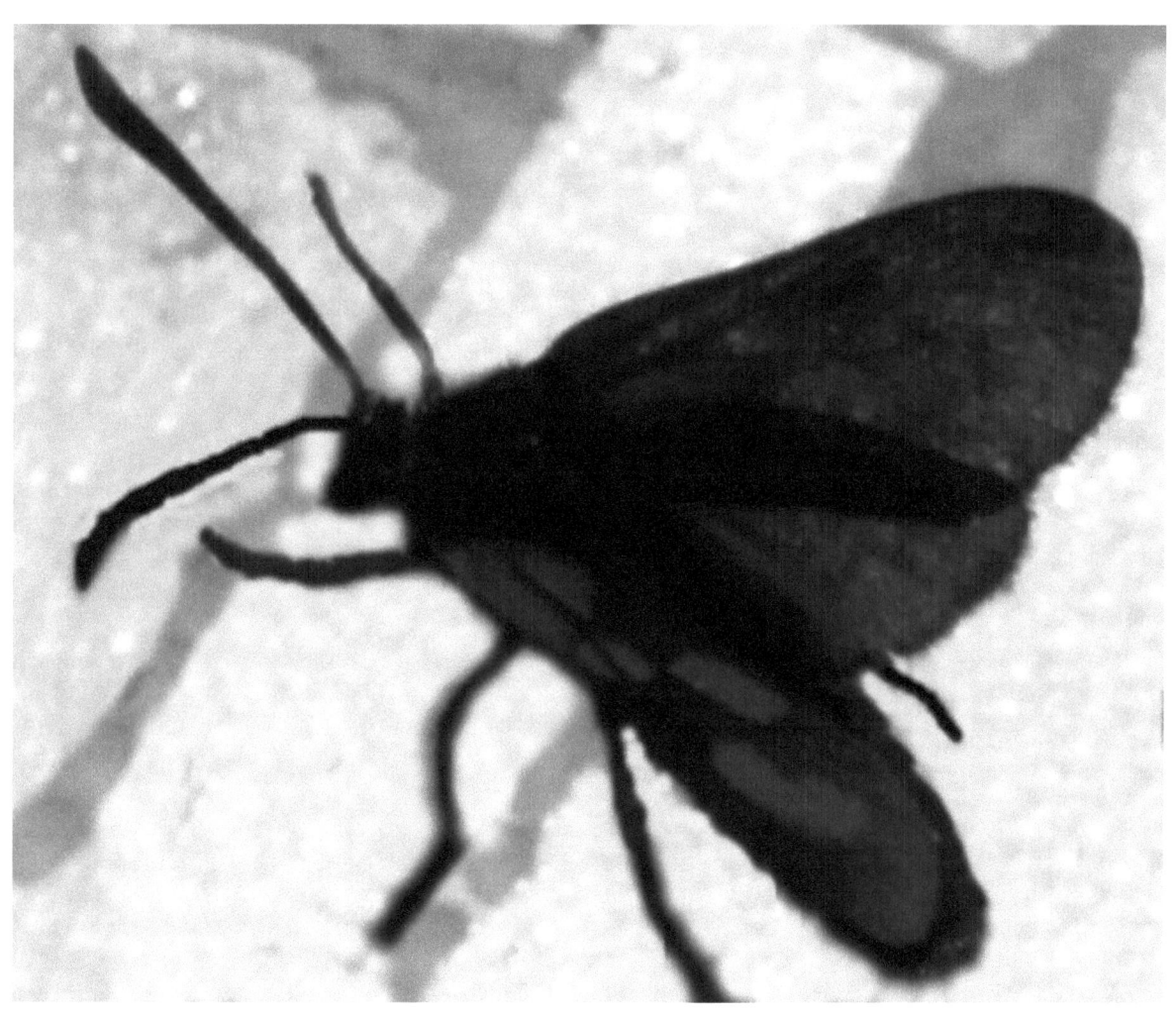

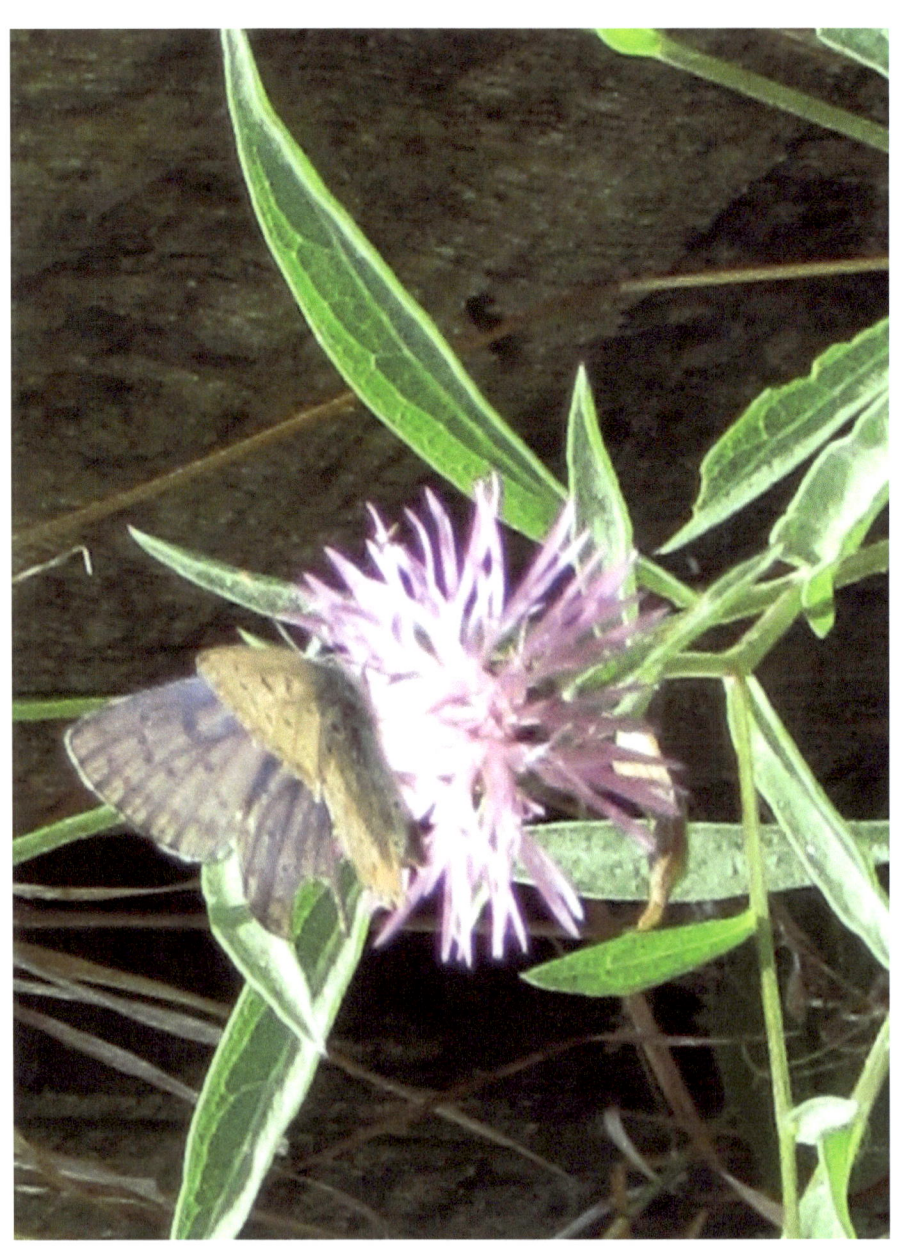

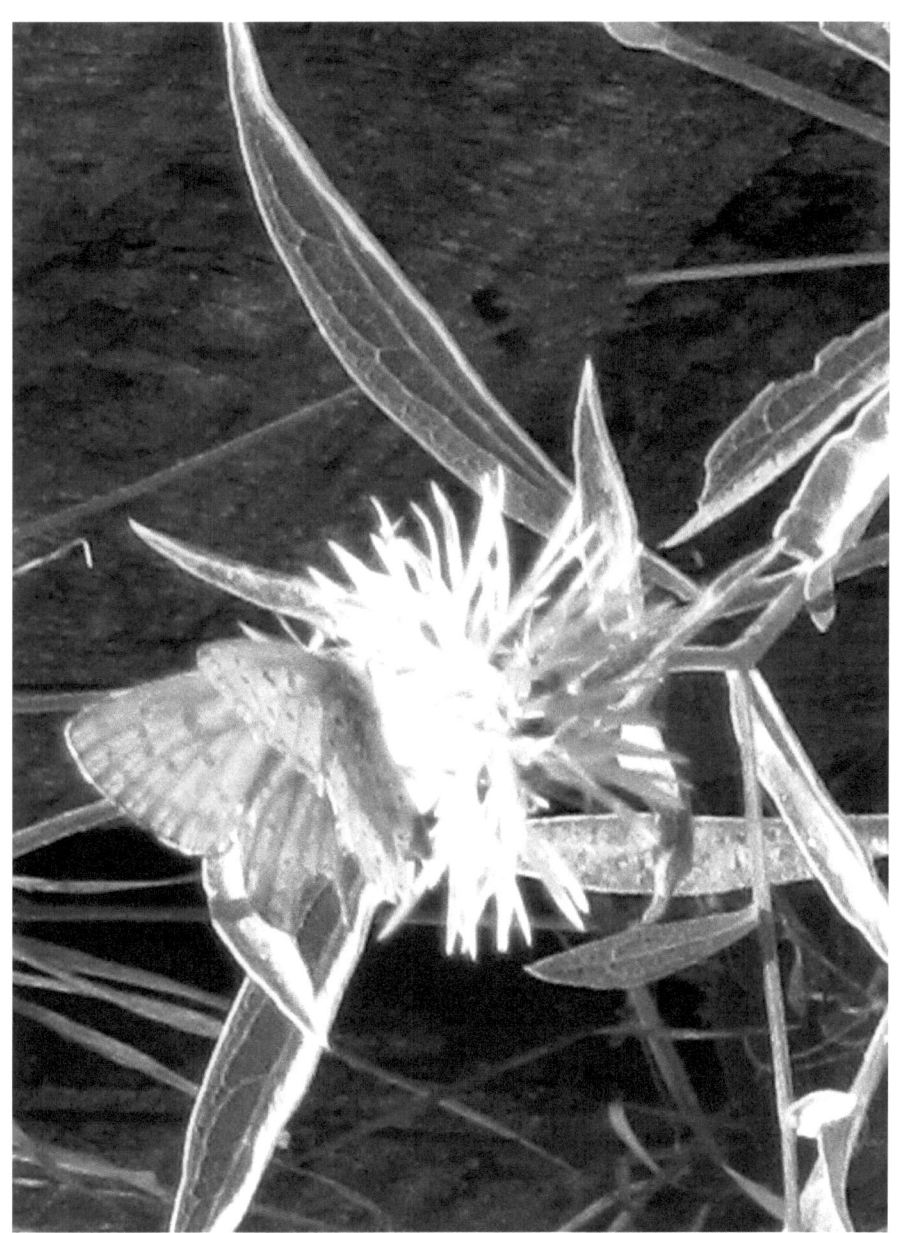

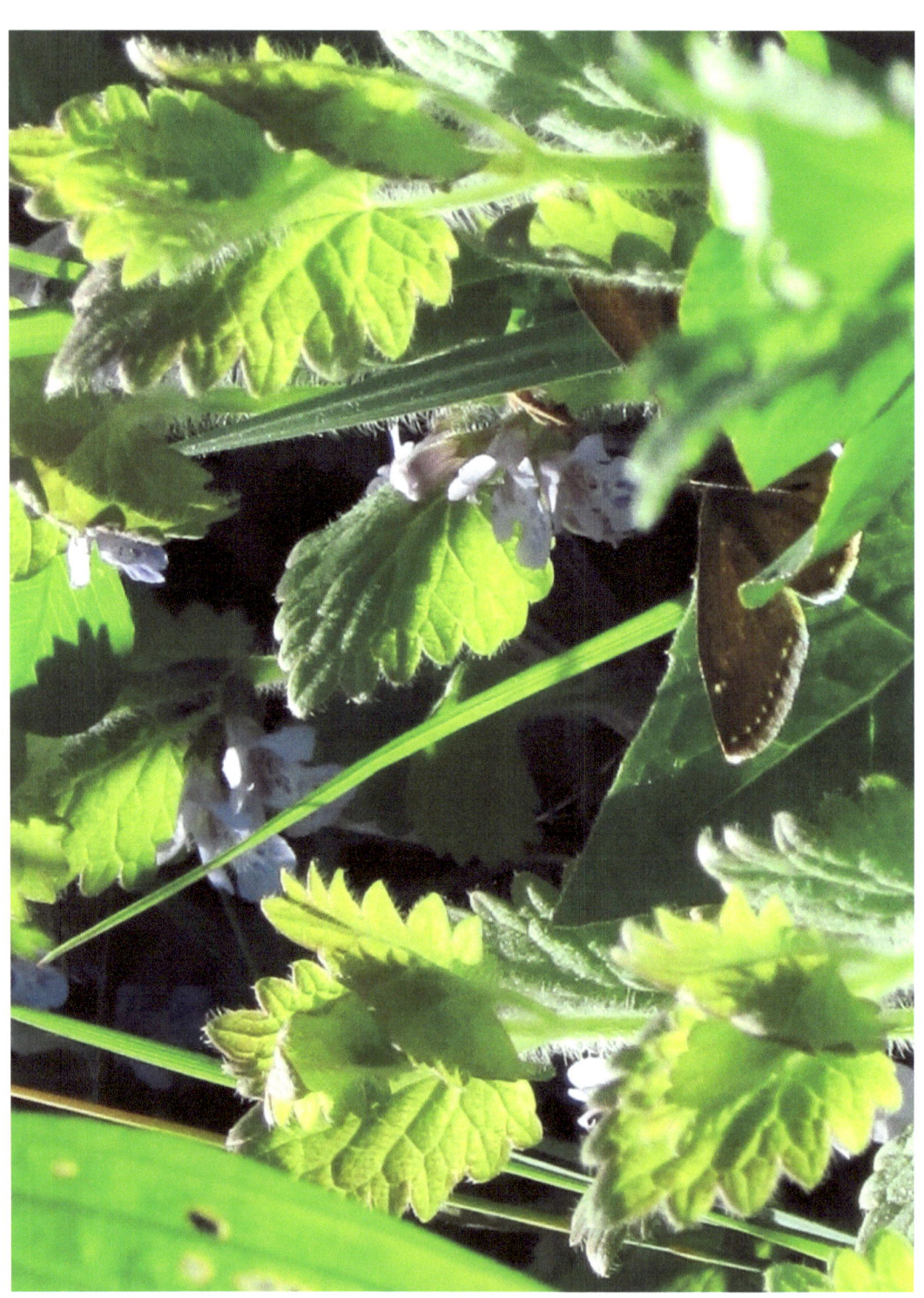

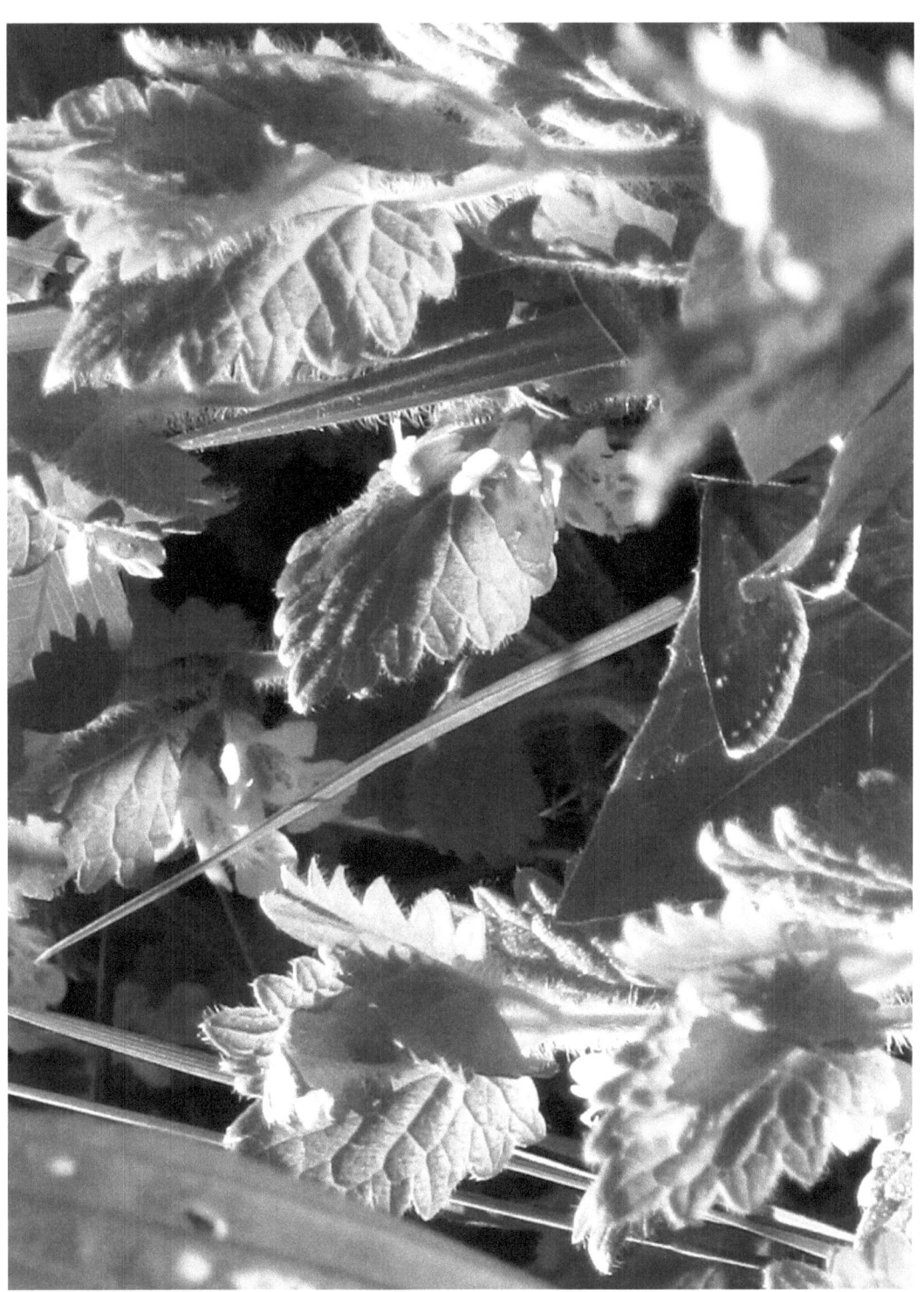

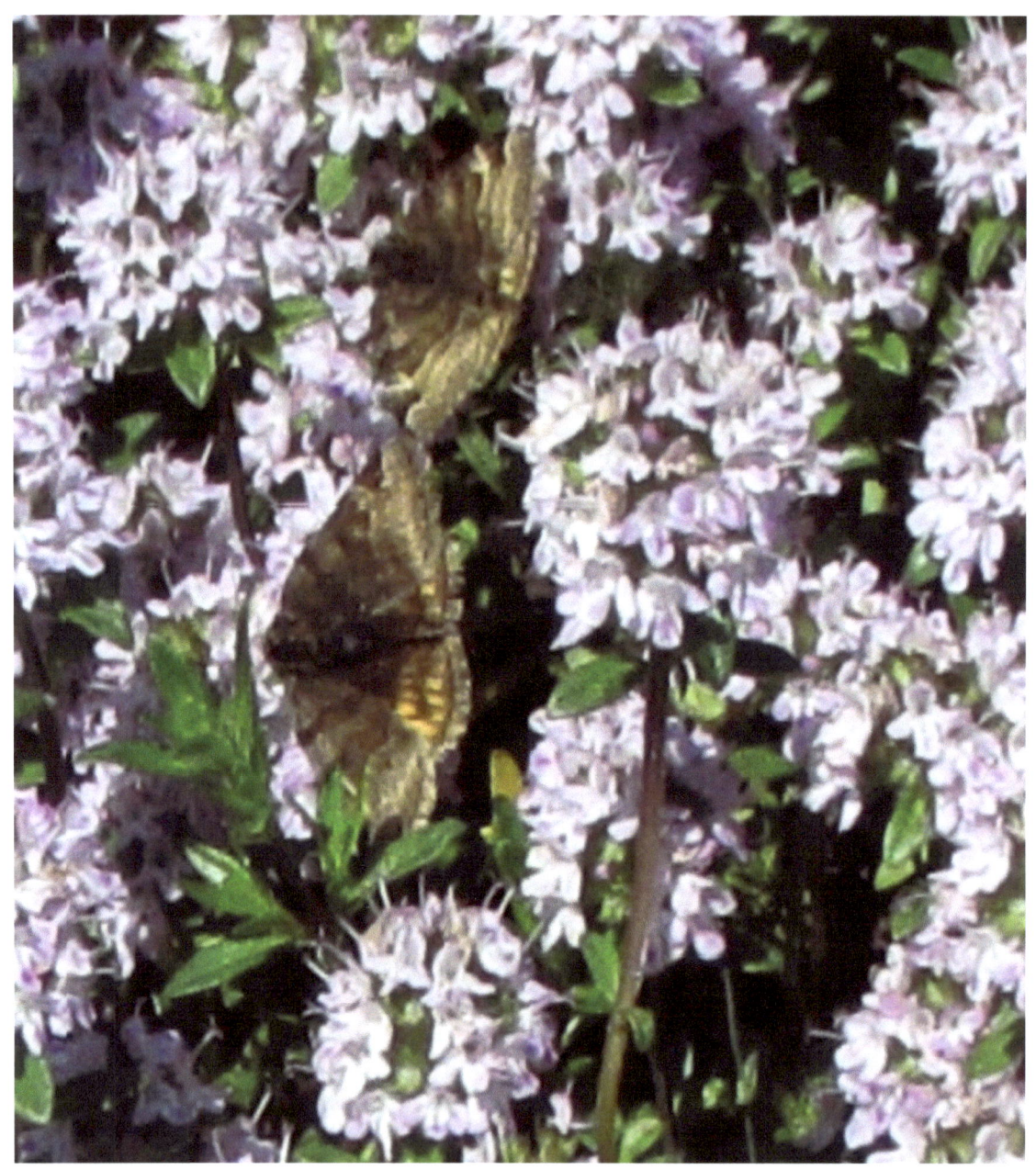

P 41

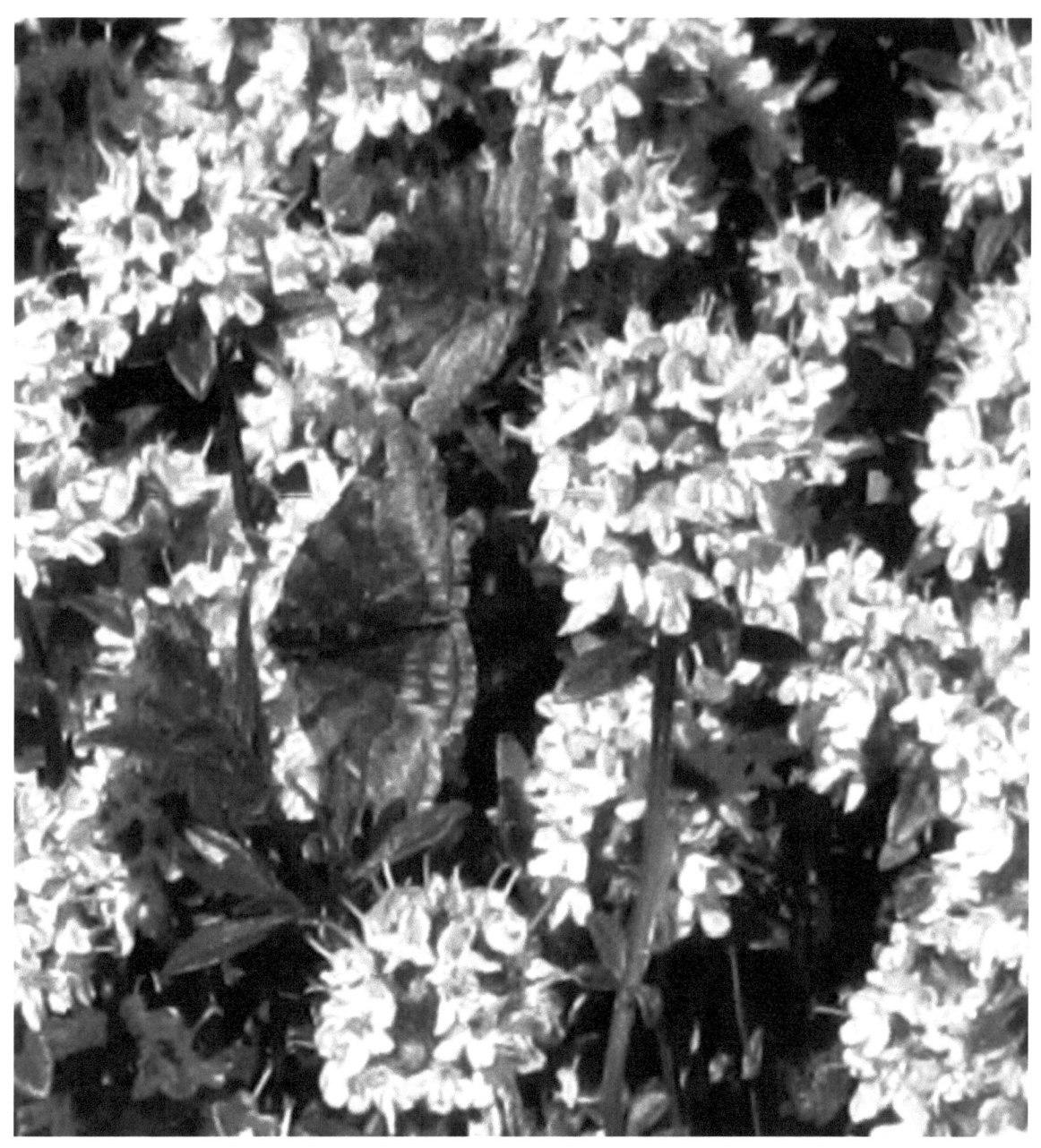

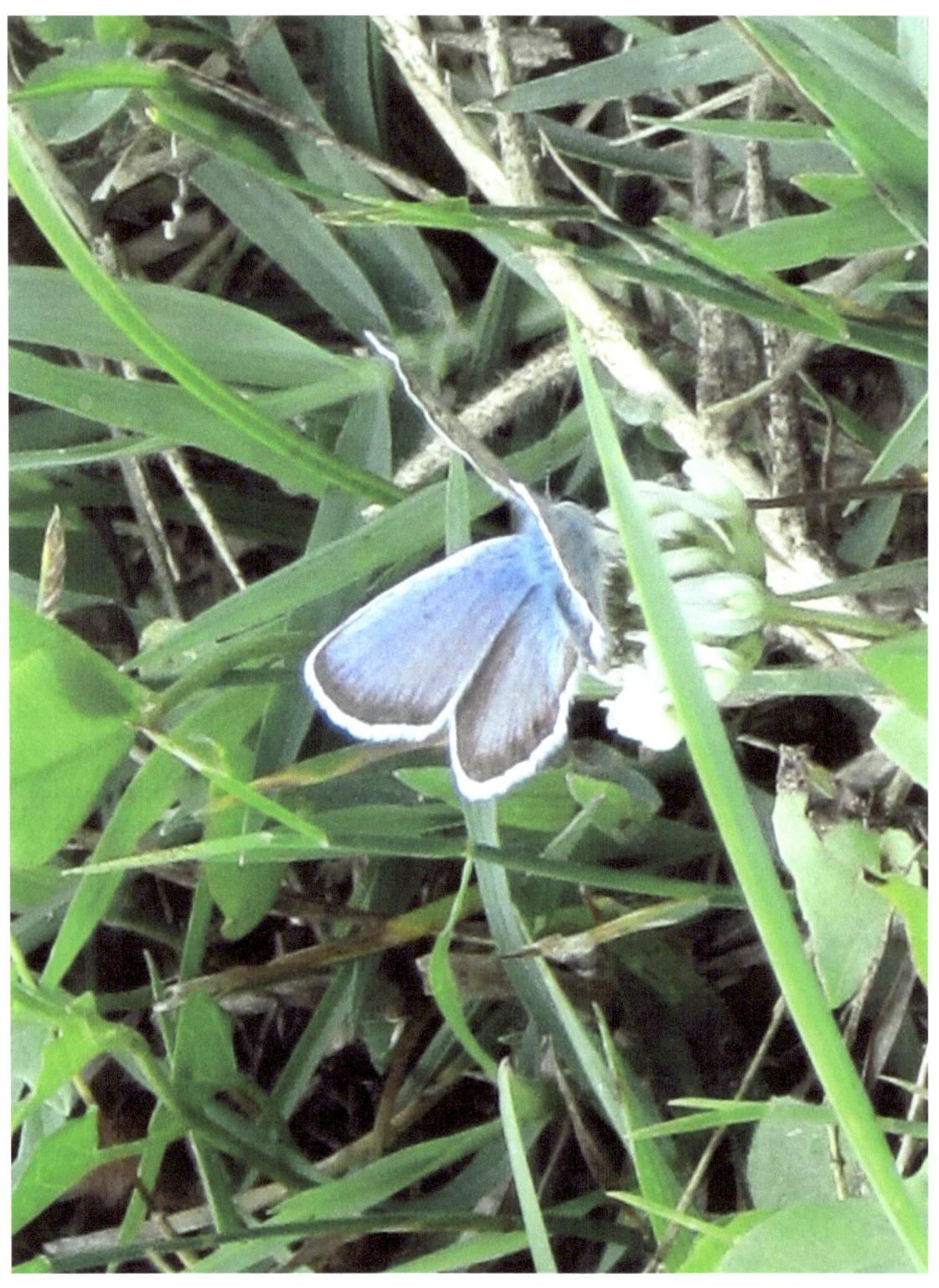

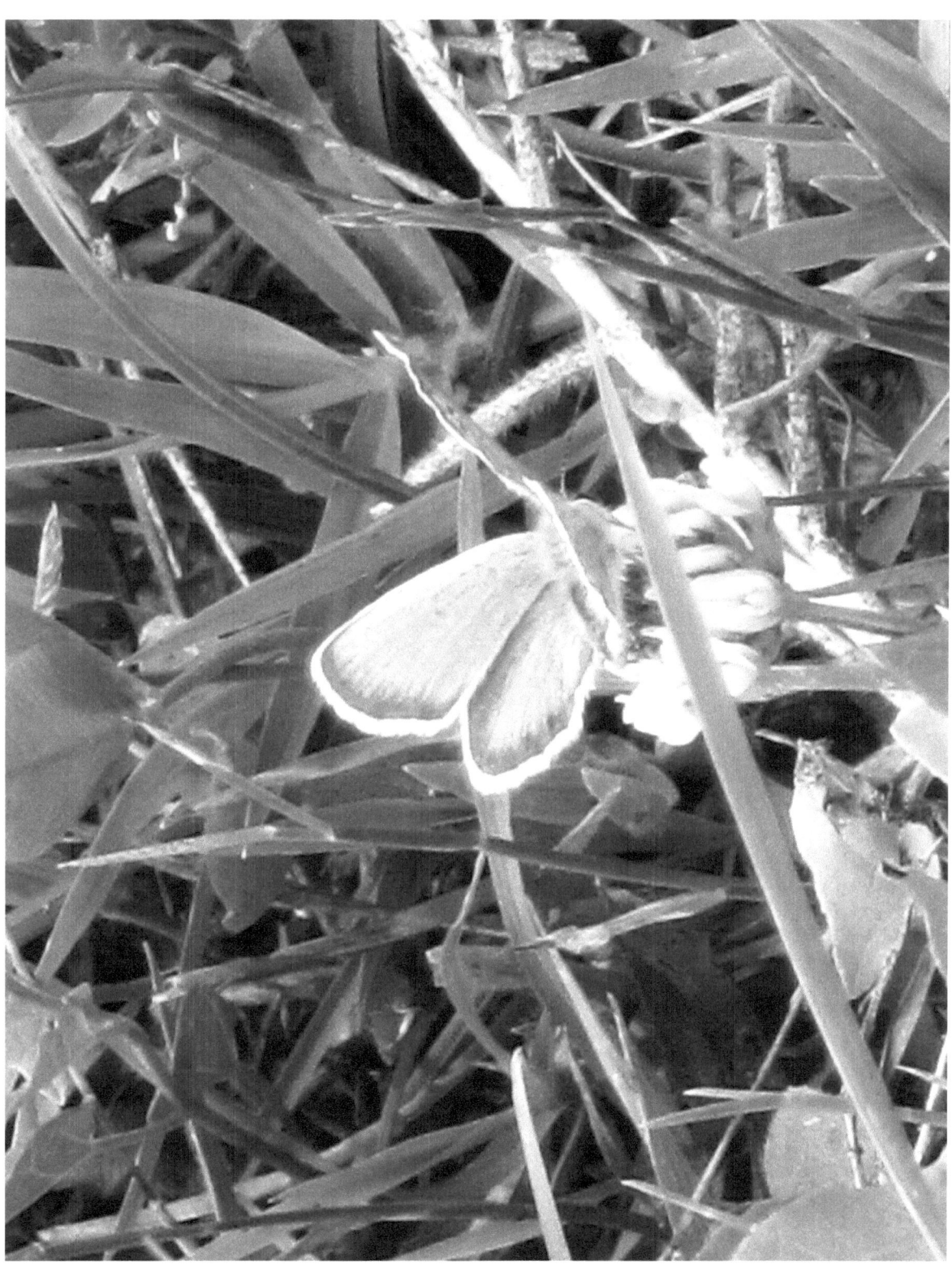

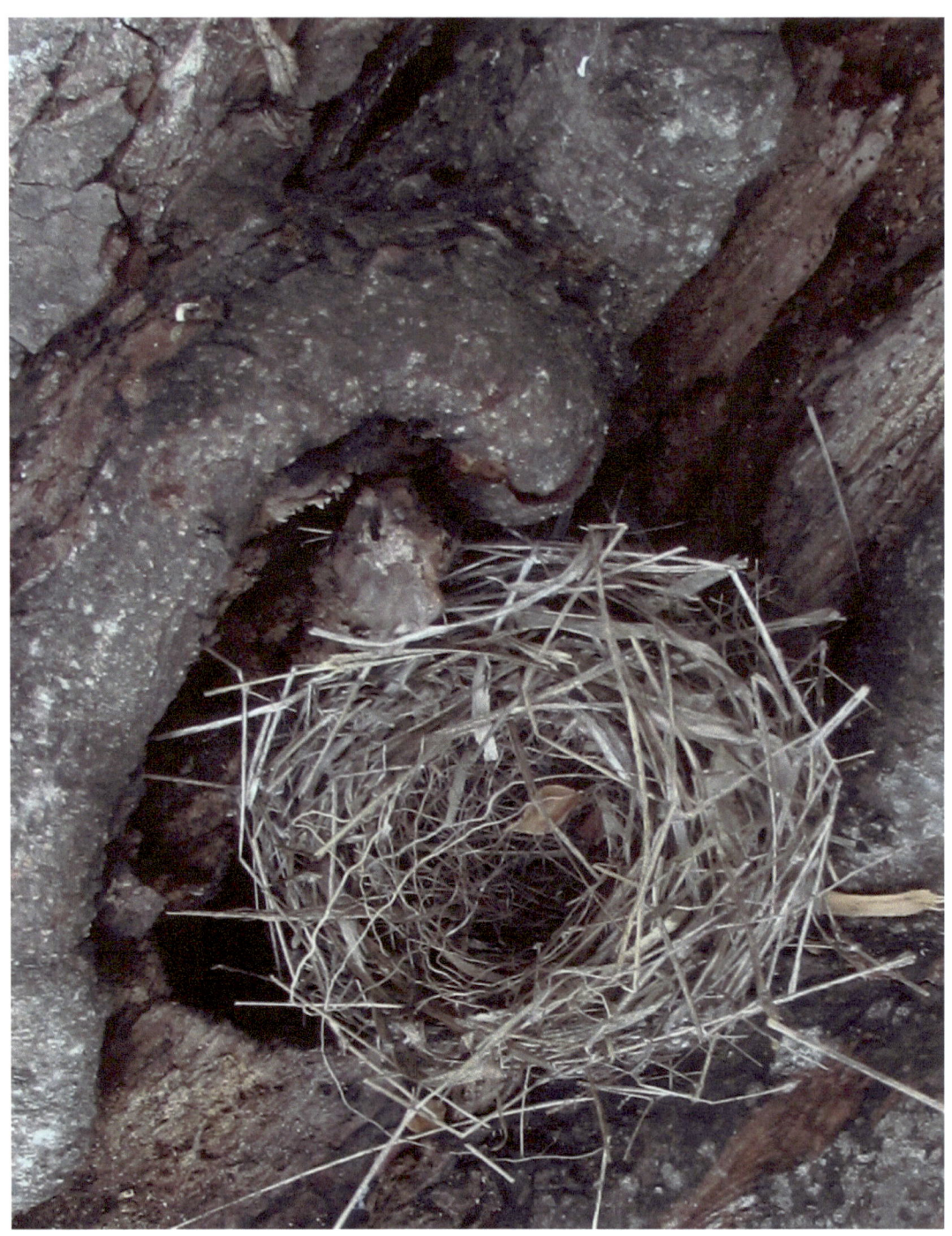

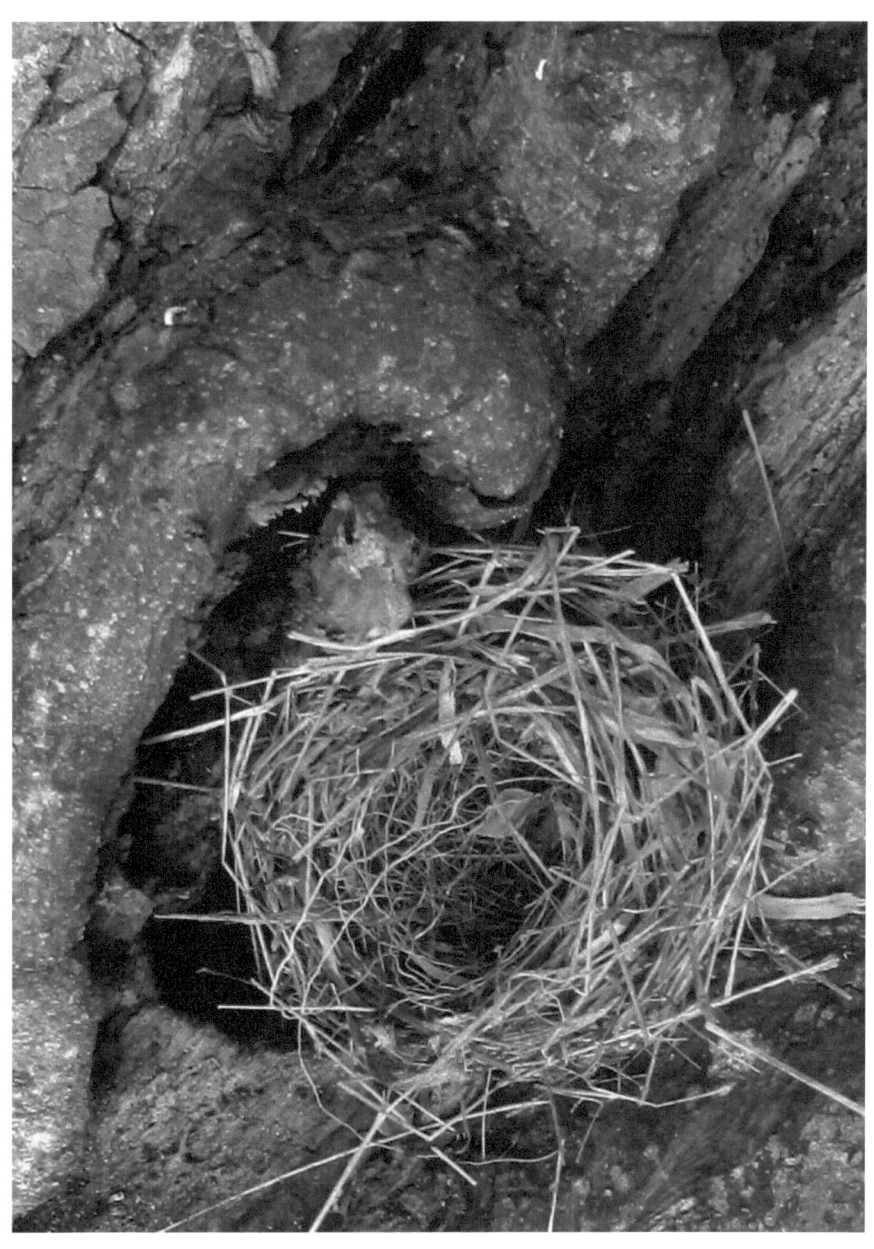

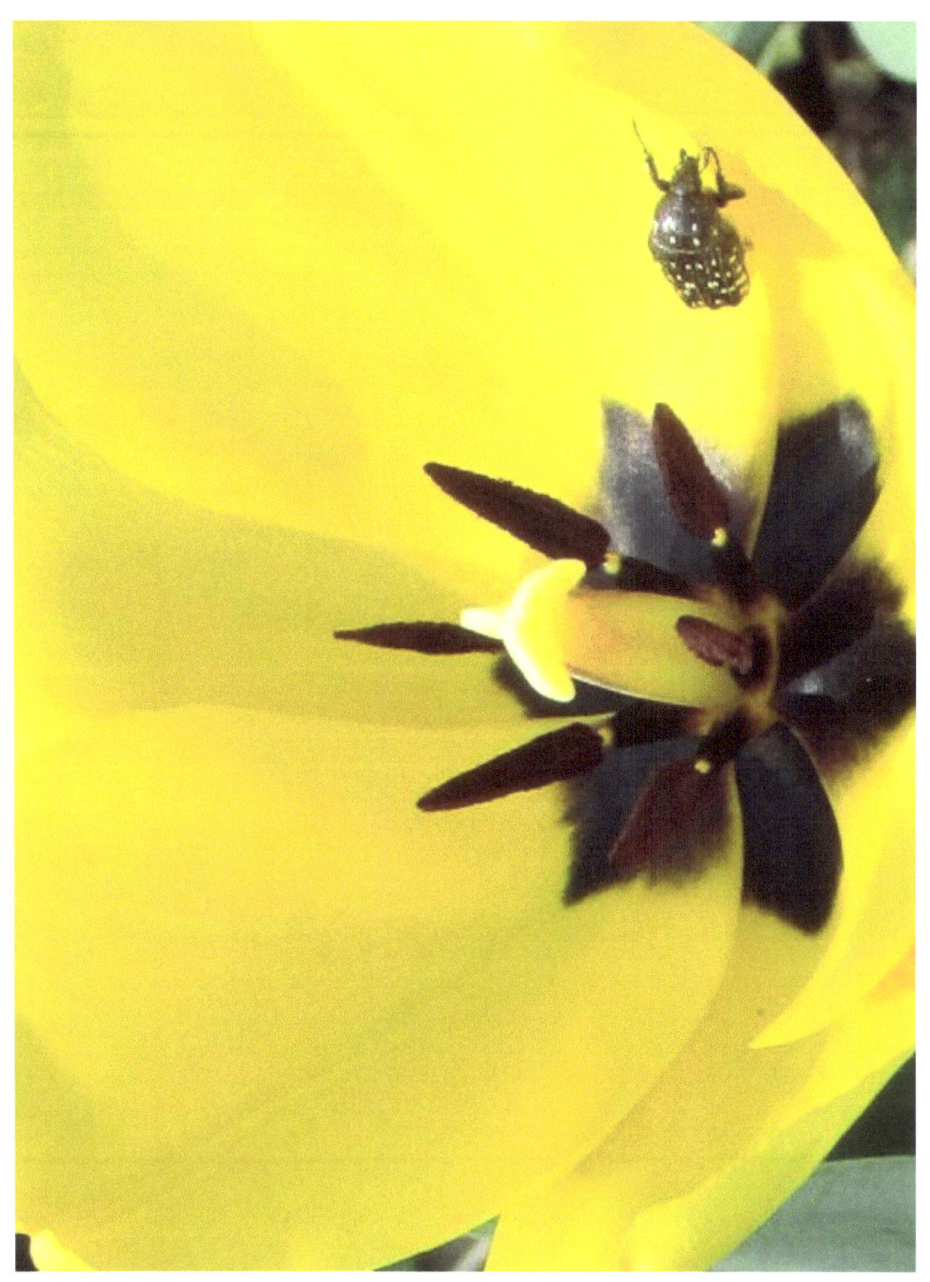

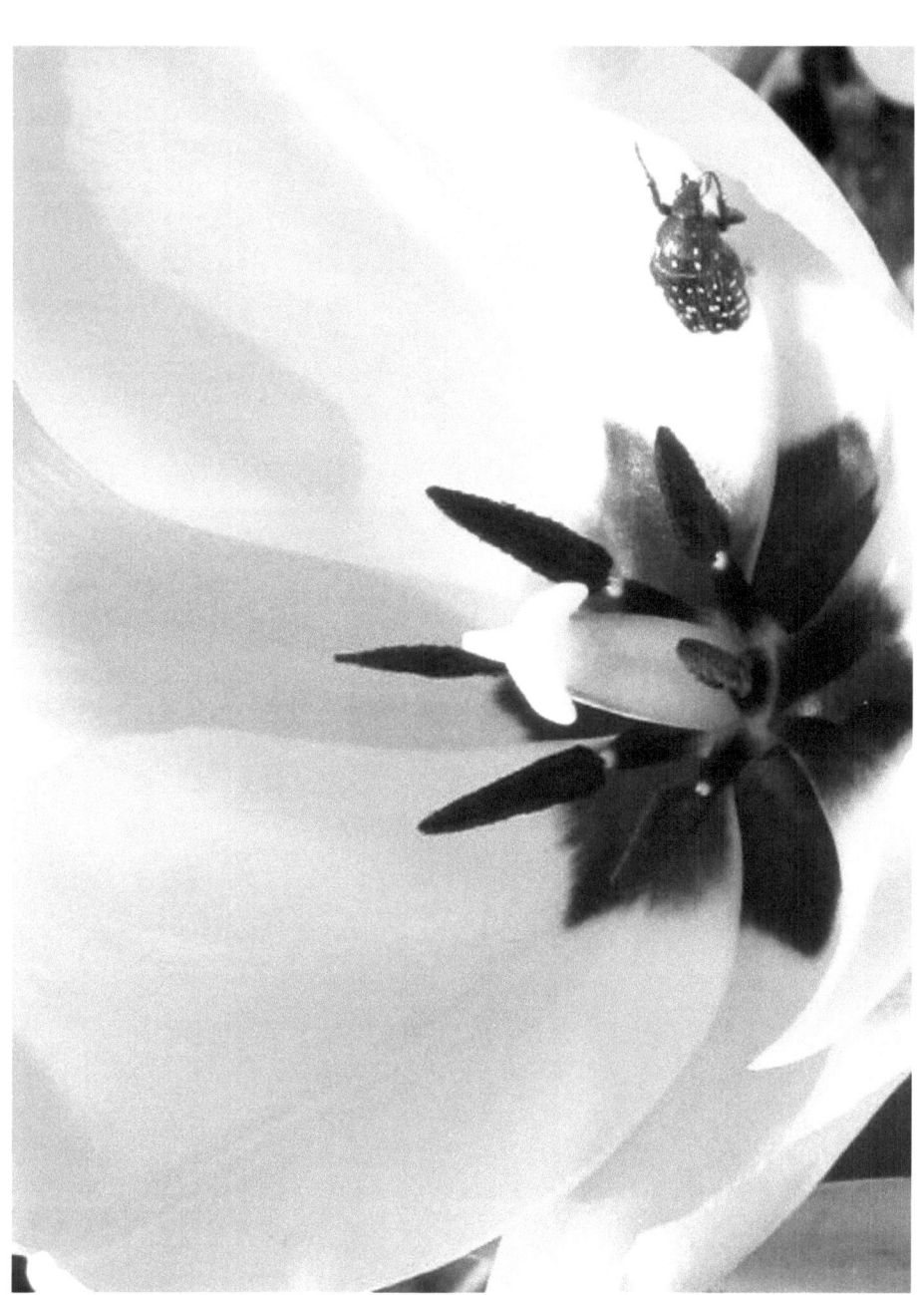

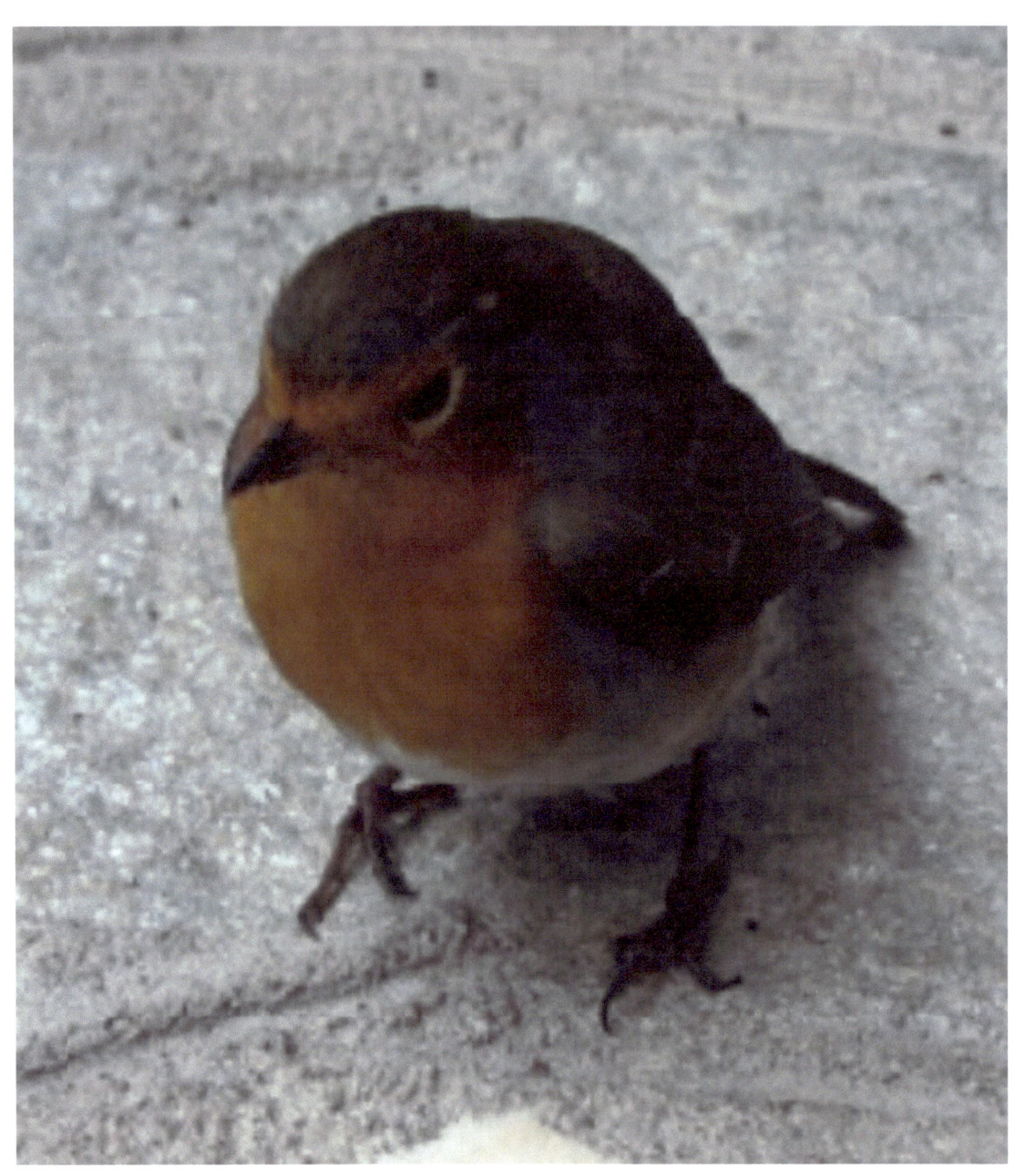

P 49

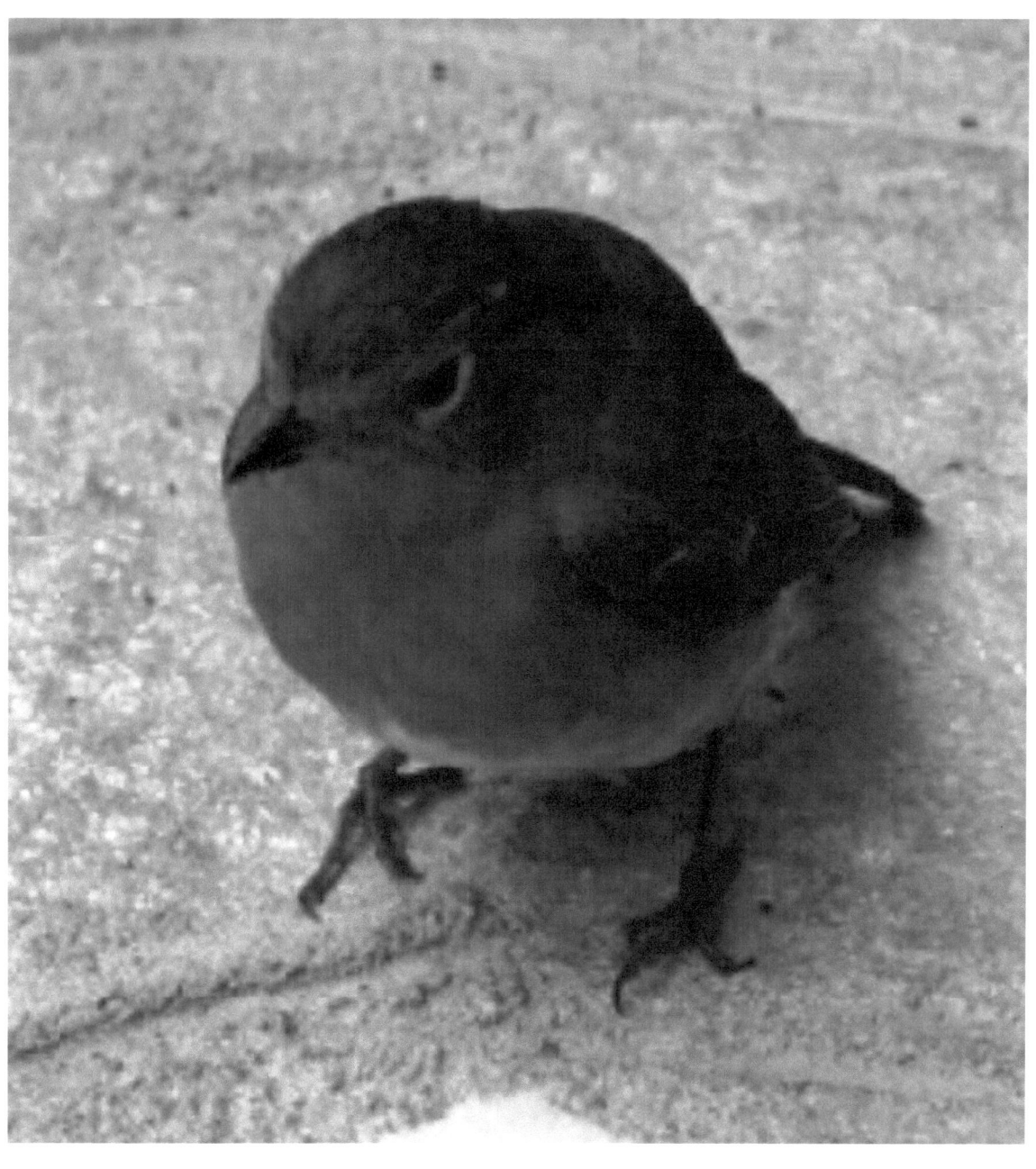

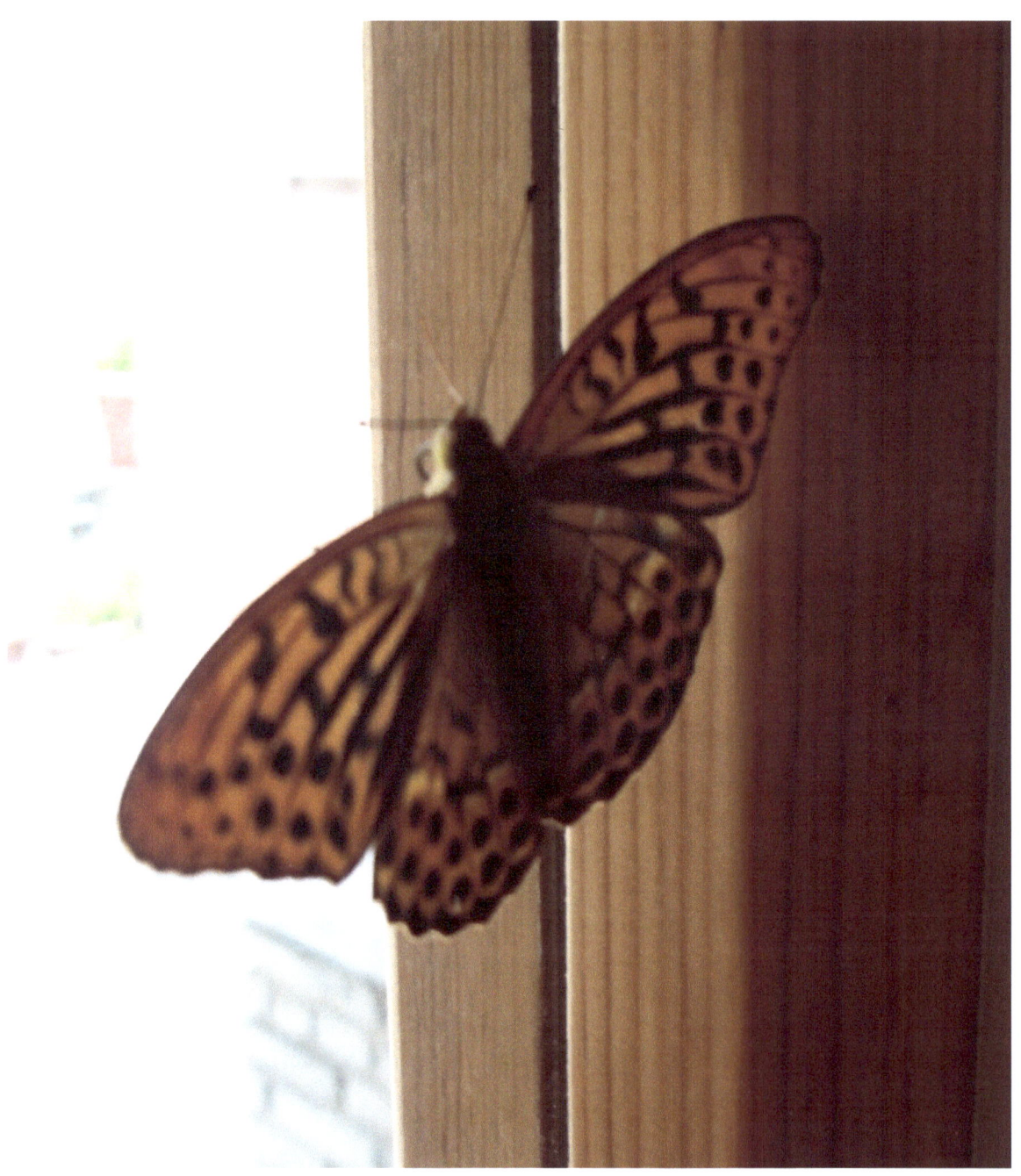

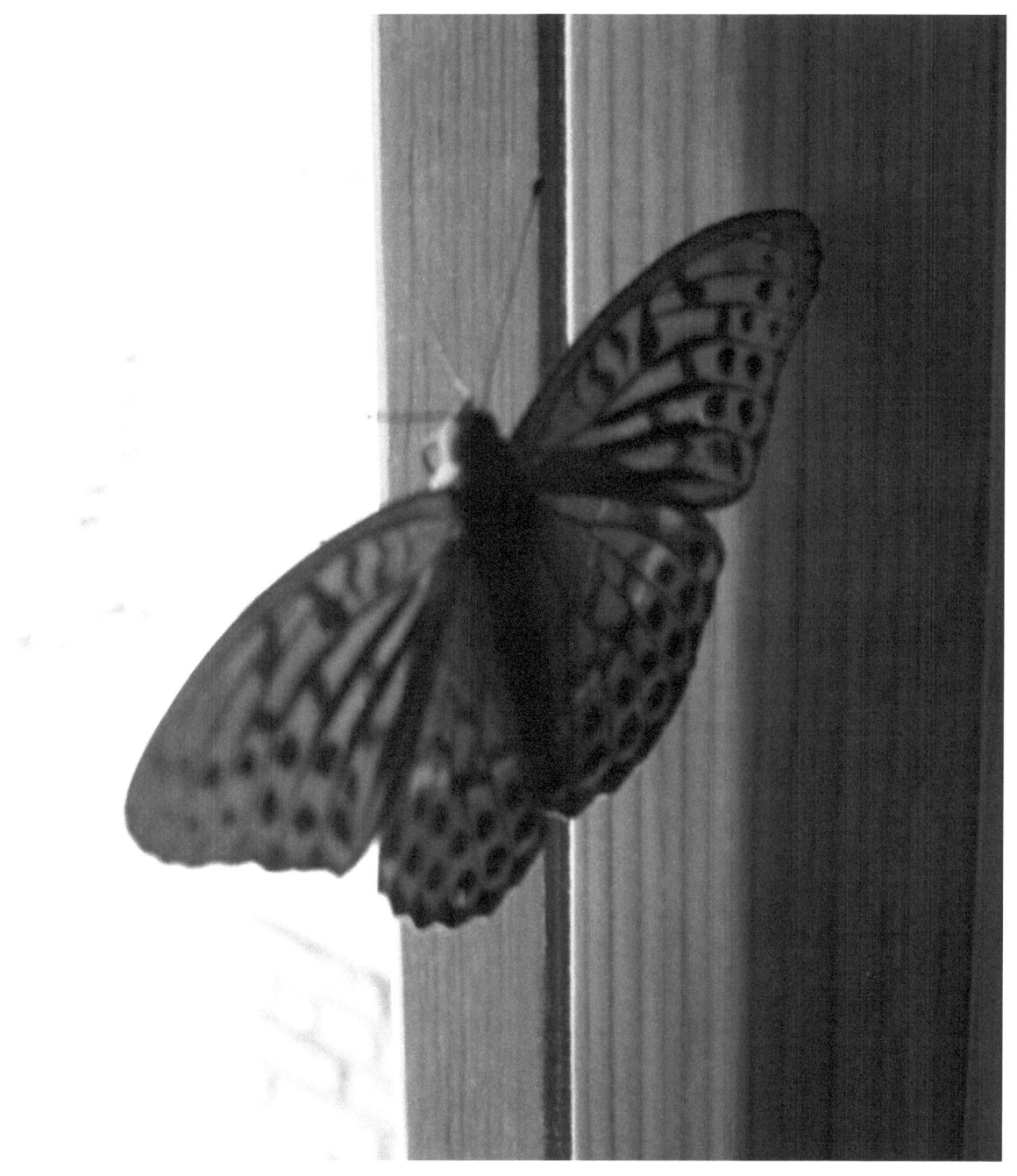

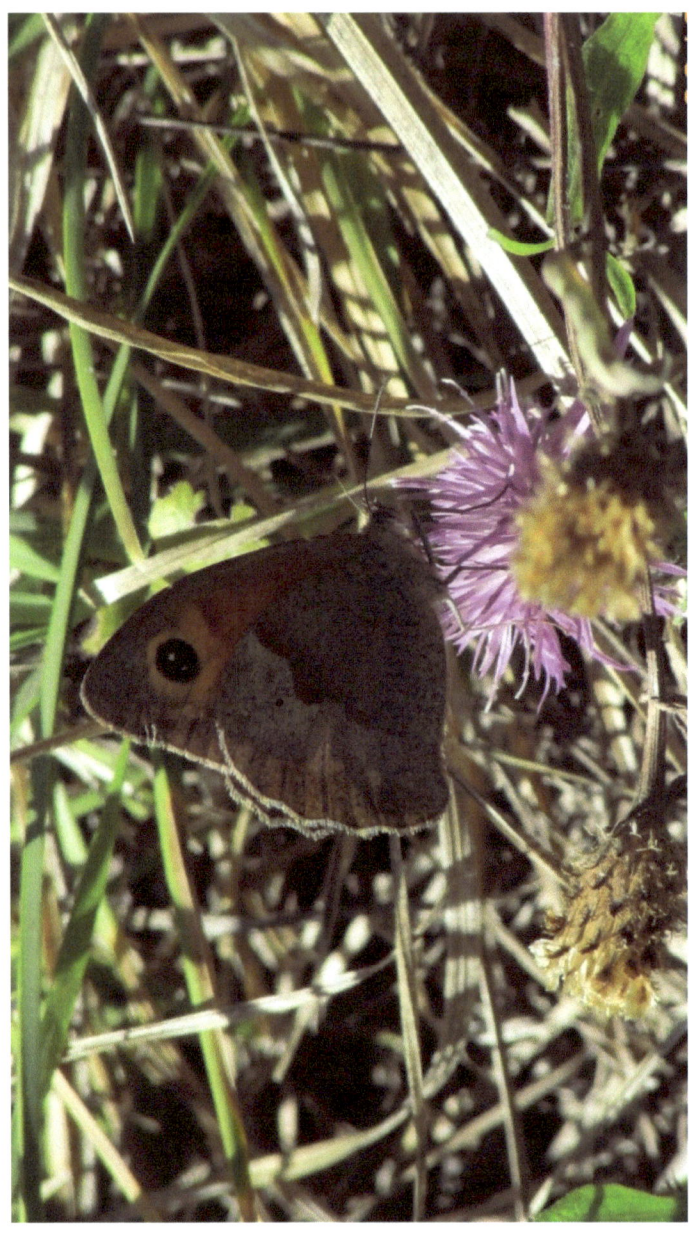

P 53

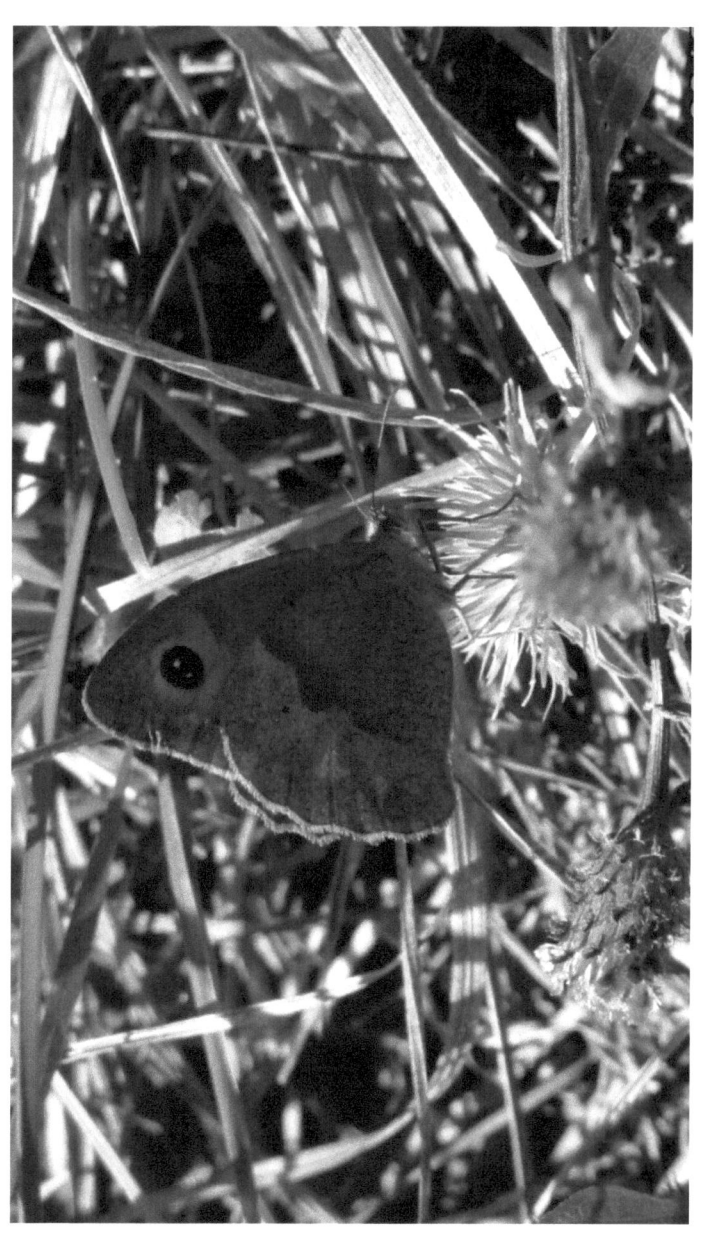

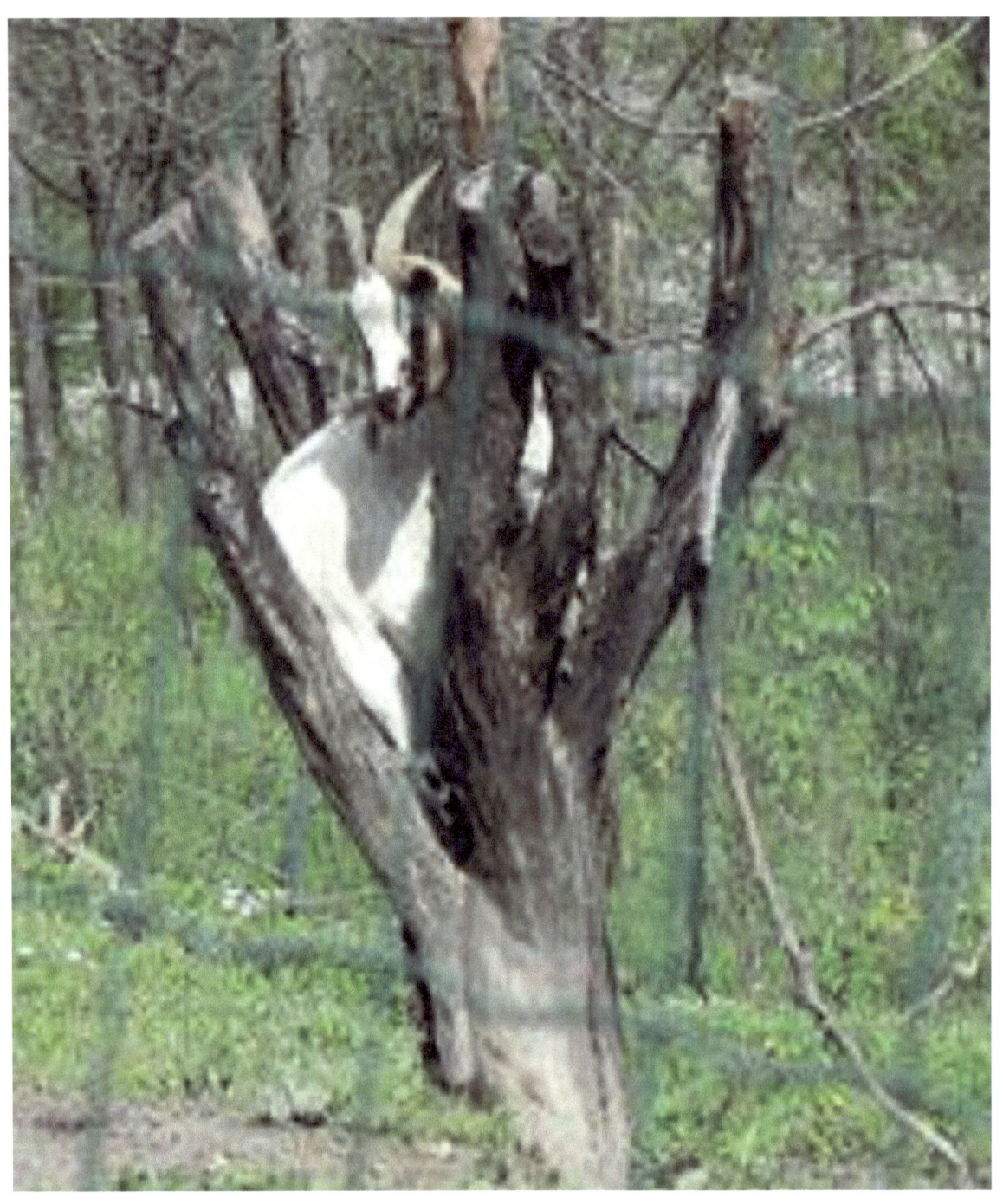

P 55

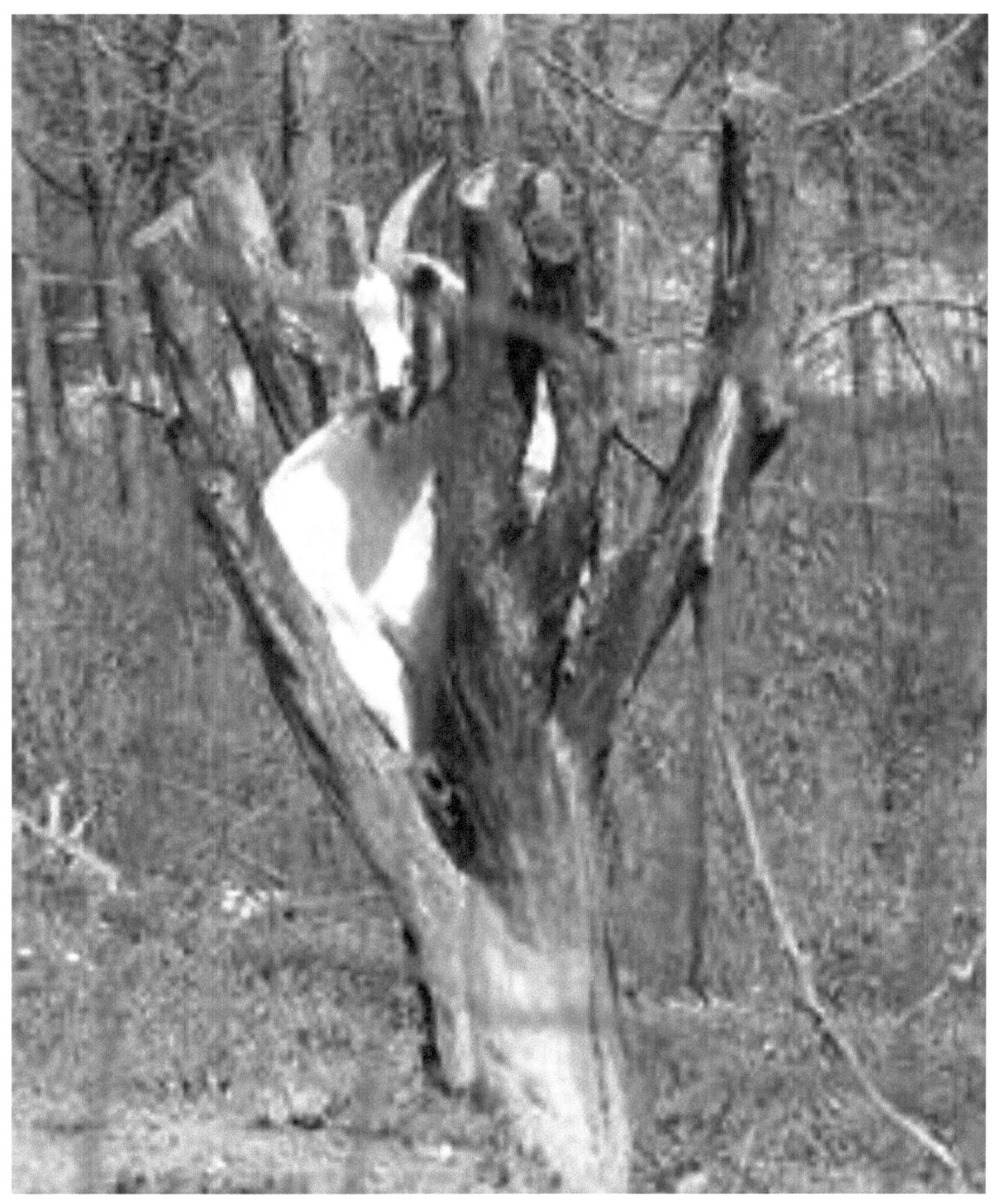

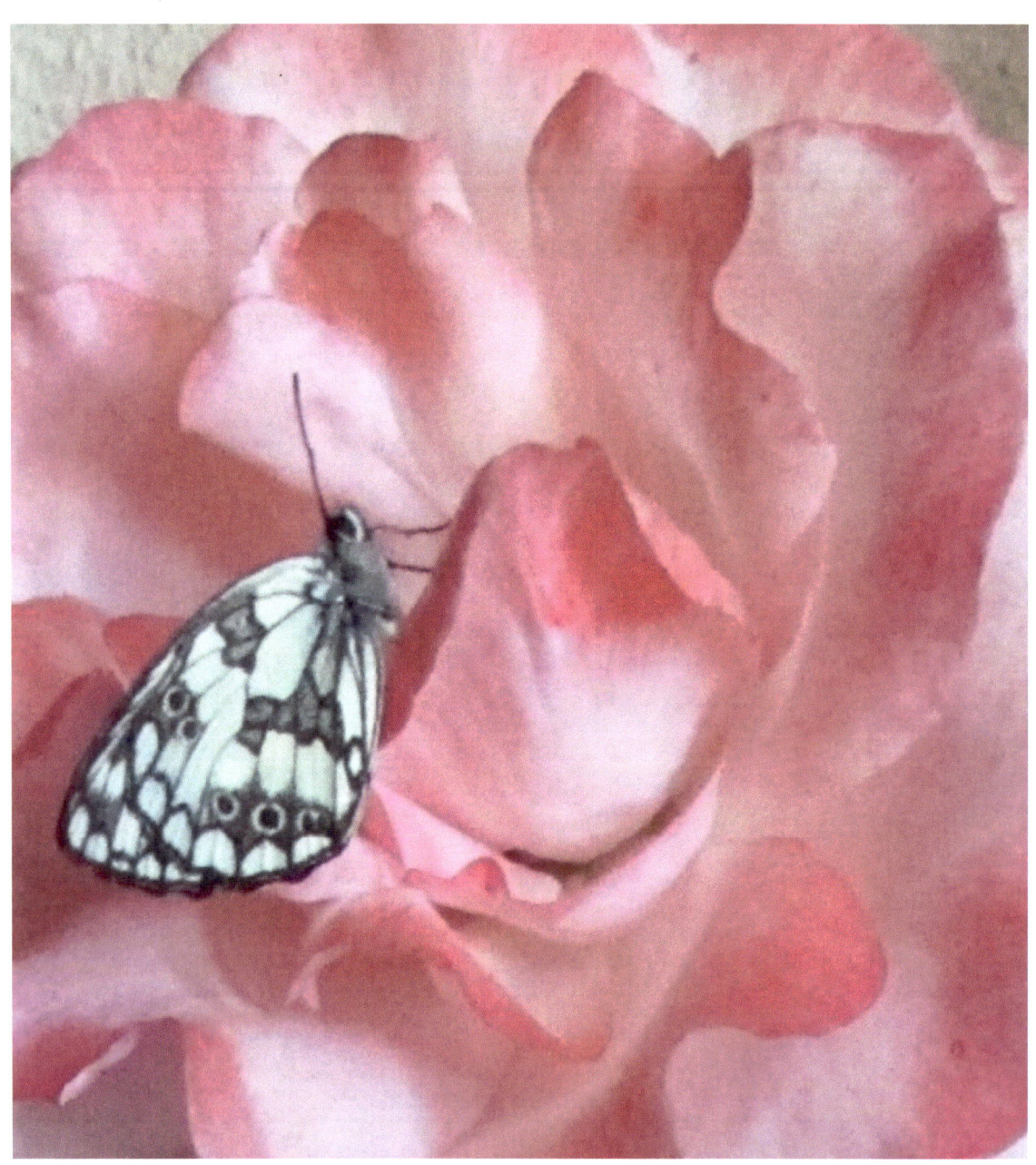

P 57

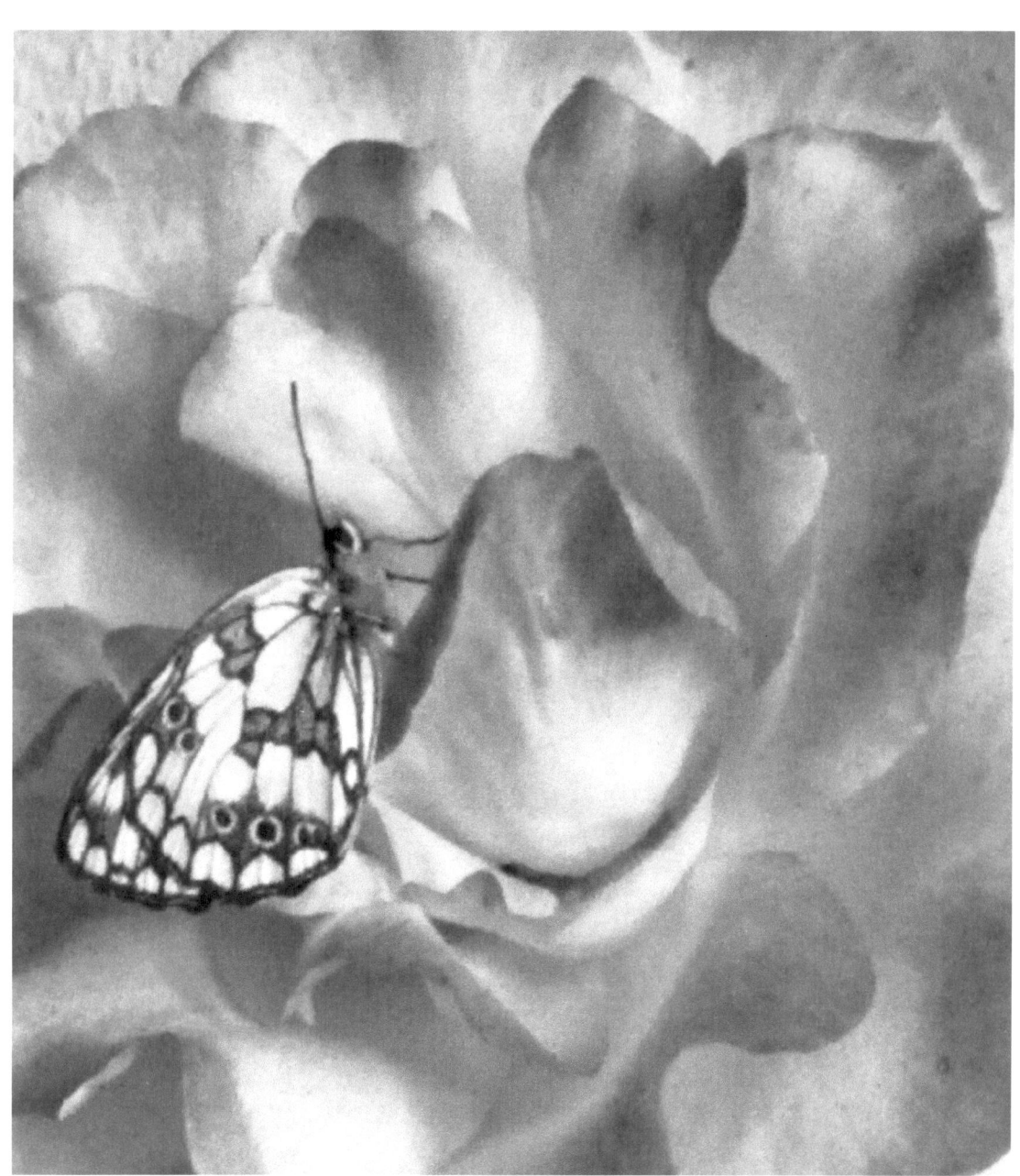

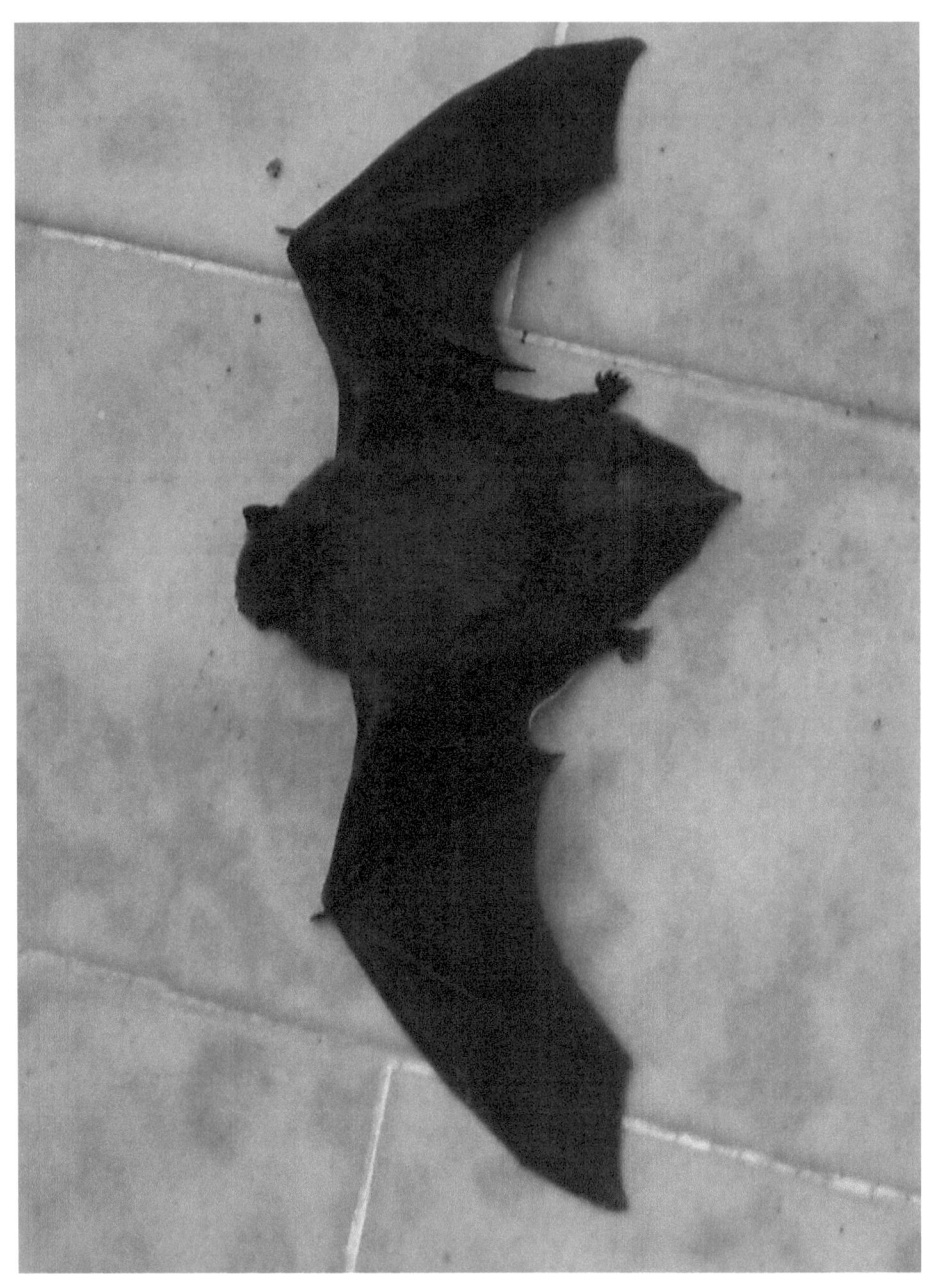

P 59

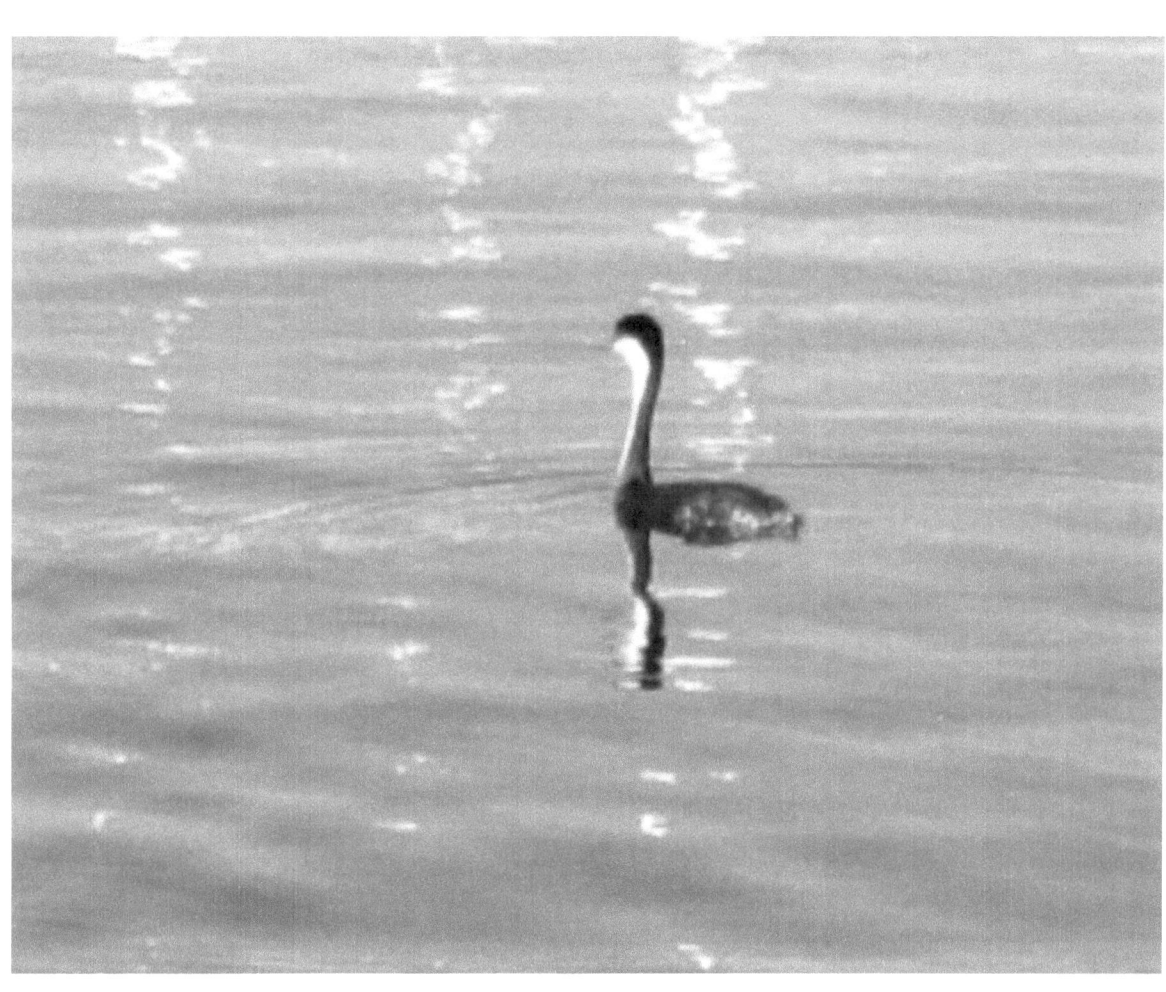

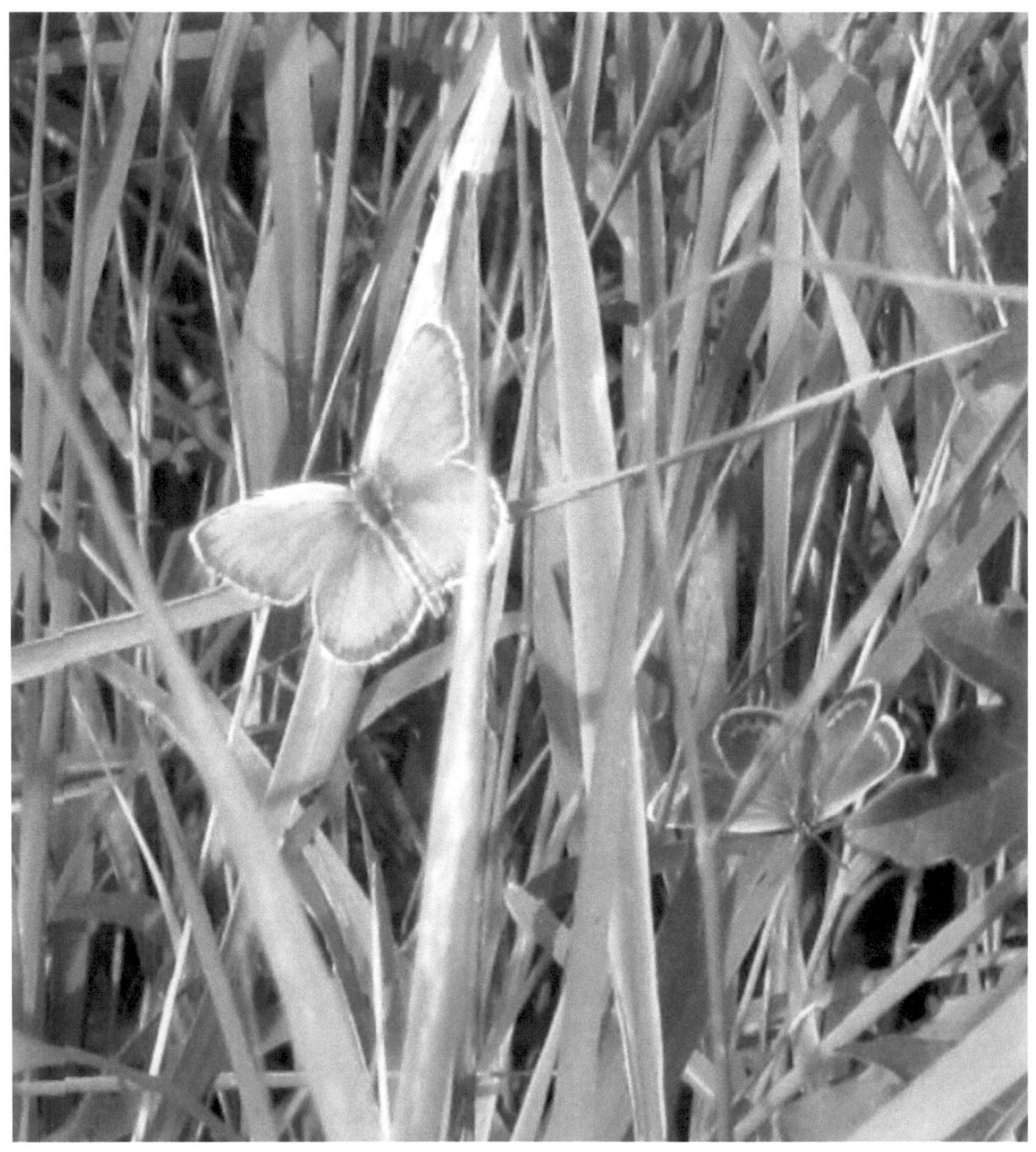

P 61

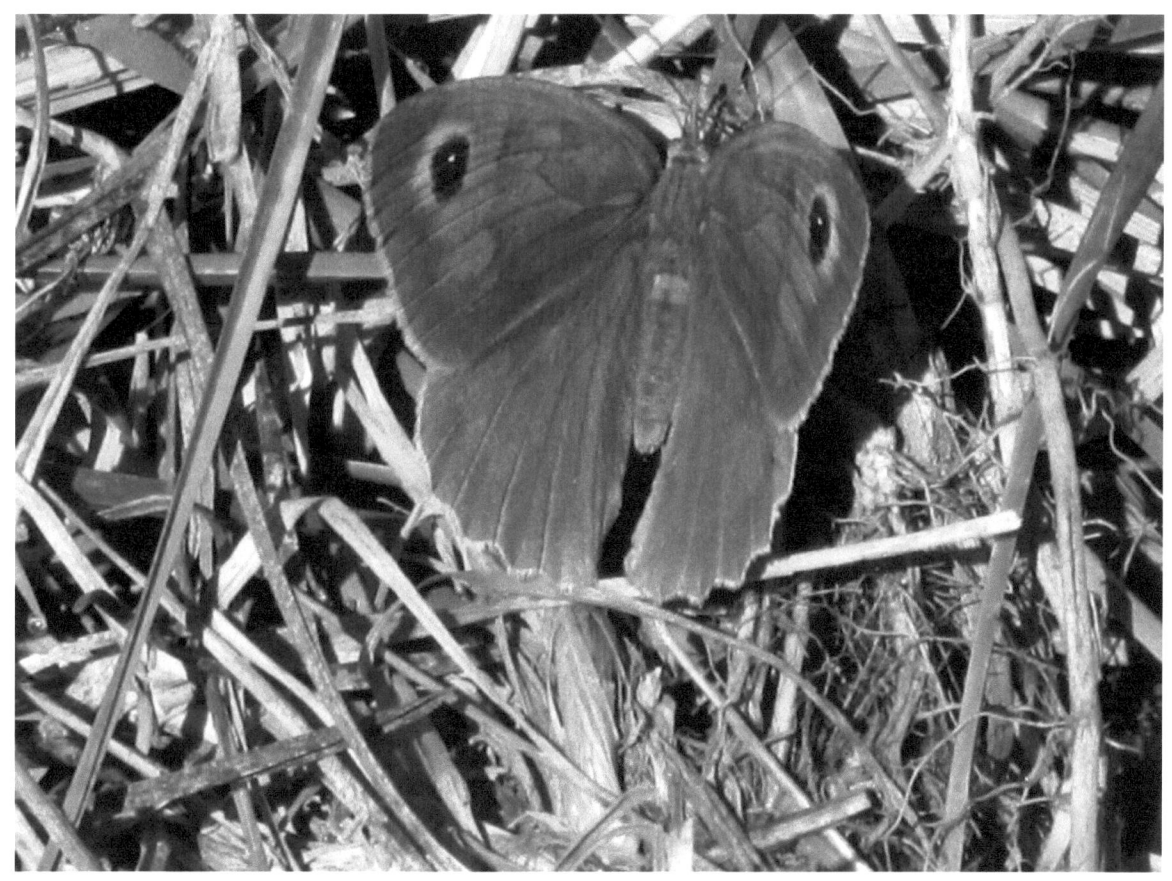

www.ingramcontent.com/pod-product-compliance
Lightning Source LLC
Chambersburg PA
CBHW041932240526
45473CB00034B/932